SHRIMAD BHAGAVAD GITA

A SEAMLESS READING

NAVEEN NIVERTHY

To Lord Krishna,

The Greatest Teacher and Best Friend.

There isn't a day that goes by without remembering you with
reverence and gratitude.

Contents

Preface

It's truly amazing how Krishna finds his way into so many aspects of Indian culture and everyday life. Whether through grand temples, lively festivals, or the simple acts of devotion in people's homes, Krishna is celebrated in countless ways. He is honored as a child, as a parent, as a lover, as a teacher, as a friend, and as the lord of all—often all at the same time. From vibrant celebrations and soulful songs to quiet moments of personal prayer, his presence touches lives in so many diverse and heartfelt ways. This deep and varied expression of love and devotion highlights not just his spiritual significance but also how he continues to inspire and connect with people across generations. Shrimad Bhagavad Gita, as the crest jewel of Krishna's teachings, stands out as a profound testament to his enduring influence and the central role he plays in the cultural and spiritual fabric of India.

The Indian spiritual tradition is rich with the timeless exchange of wisdom between teacher and student, where the deepest truths of life are passed down through heartfelt dialogue. Shrimad Bhagavad Gita is one such dialogue. Shrimad means 'glorious' or 'auspicious', emphasizes the reverence and grandeur associated with the text. Bhagavad refers to 'the Lord', specifically Lord Krishna, who imparts the wisdom in the Gita, while Gita means "song." Thus, Shrimad Bhagavad Gita translates to 'The Glorious Song of the Lord'. The use of Shrimad elevates the Gita, reminding us that it holds timeless guidance for living a meaningful life and attaining spiritual liberation, making it worthy of deep respect and reverence. However, this is not the only Gita found within the epic Mahabharata. In fact, there are several Gitas, each offering unique insights into the human experience, though none are as widely revered as the Bhagavad Gita.

For example, there's the 'Anu Gita', a conversation that takes place after the great war, where Arjuna, still hungry for knowledge, asks Krishna to recapitulate the teachings of the Bhagavad Gita. This dialogue is found in the Ashvamedhika Parva of the Mahabharata. Then there's the 'Uddhava Gita', where Krishna shares his final teachings with his dear devotee Uddhava, focusing on the path of devotion and renunciation, a touching farewell before Krishna leaves the earthly realm.

Other Gitas within the Mahabharata include the 'Ashtavakra Gita', a powerful discourse between the sage Ashtavakra and King Janaka, exploring the nature of self and the essence of non-duality, and the 'Brahmana Gita', a poignant exchange between a Brahmana and his wife, discussing detachment and the fleeting nature of worldly life.

But among all these, the Bhagavad Gita stands out as the most comprehensive and profound. In Mahabharata, Arjuna's deep despair on the battlefield of Kurukshetra became the starting point for his profound self-reflection. Faced with a moral dilemma about fighting his own family, he was overcome with grief and confusion, unable to act. In this moment of vulnerability, he turned to Krishna for guidance, asking fundamental questions about life, duty, and the self. This enquiry led to the teachings of the Bhagavad Gita, where Krishna revealed timeless wisdom , helping Arjuna rise above his sorrow. It's more than just a conversation; it's a complete guide to life, offering wisdom on duty, righteousness, devotion, and the nature of reality itself. It's no wonder that the Bhagavad Gita, found in the

Bhishma Parva of the Mahabharata (chapters 23 to 40), has been cherished as a spiritual classic for centuries.

Initially, the Gita was studied as part of the Mahabharata, but over time, its profound significance as a standalone text became increasingly recognized. In the 8th century CE, Adi Shankaracharya, one of India's greatest spiritual teachers, wrote the first major commentary on the Gita, interpreting its teachings through the lens of Advaita Vedanta, the philosophy of non-dualism. His work laid the groundwork for generations of spiritual seekers.

As centuries passed, other great thinkers added their own perspectives. Ramanuja, in the 11th century, saw the Gita through the eyes of devotion, emphasizing the relationship between the individual and the divine in his 'Gita Bhasya'. Madhvacharya, in the 13th century, presented a dualistic view in his commentary 'Gita Tattva', highlighting the distinction between the soul and the supreme reality. Nimbarka, a century later, introduced a philosophy that balanced both unity and difference in the divine.

In the 15th century, the Bhakti movement, led by figures like Chaitanya Mahaprabhu, brought the Gita's teachings to the masses, focusing on the path of devotion. And as the Gita's influence spread beyond India, English translations in the 18th and 19th centuries by scholars like Charles Wilkins and Edwin Arnold introduced this spiritual masterpiece to the world.

The Gita's teachings have inspired countless individuals, from Mahatma Gandhi, who called it his 'spiritual dictionary', to Sri Aurobindo, who delved deep into its metaphysical aspects in his 'Essays on the Gita'. Bal Gangadhar Tilak interpreted it as a call to selfless action, writing his famous "Gita Rahasya" while imprisoned by the

British.

Even beyond India, the Gita's wisdom has touched the hearts of many. Aldous Huxley saw it as a work of perennial philosophy, while J. Robert Oppenheimer, the physicist behind the atomic bomb, famously quoted the Gita after witnessing the first nuclear explosion: 'Now I am become Death, the destroyer of worlds.'

The Bhagavad Gita continues to resonate with people across the globe, offering timeless guidance on how to live a meaningful life. Its teachings are as relevant today as they were thousands of years ago, making it a truly universal scripture.

Why another book on Bhagavad Gita?

The Bhagavad Gita is a masterpiece of spiritual wisdom. There's so much fluidity, clarity, and simplicity in its teachings that it can be overwhelming at times. I firmly believe that if there were only one traditional text that we could prescribe as 'enough' to lead to liberation, it would be this one. Shrimad Bhagavad Gita is revered as both 'Brahmavidya' (the science of the ultimate reality, Brahman) and 'Yoga Shastra' (a scripture on the practice of spiritual discipline). As Brahmavidya, the Gita offers profound teachings on the nature of the all pervasive Self (Atma) and the limitless absolute reality (Brahman), guiding seekers toward the knowledge of their true, eternal essence beyond the transient body and mind. It expounds on the highest wisdom that liberates one from the cycle of birth and death. This knowledge is not merely theoretical but actionable and deeply transformative, leading to the realization of the Self as free, whole, and infinite.

At the same time, the Gita is a Yoga Shastra, a practical guide to spiritual evolution through the disciplined integration of action, devotion, meditation and self-knowledge. While terms like Karma Yoga (the yoga of action), Bhakti Yoga (the yoga of devotion), and Jnana Yoga (the yoga of knowledge) are often used, they are not separate or distinct paths in the Gita. Krishna teaches that these are interconnected facets of the same spiritual journey. Karma Yoga purifies the mind by encouraging selfless action without attachment to results, preparing one for the knowledge of the Self. Bhakti Yoga, devotion to the divine, dissolves the ego and cultivates surrender, which complements the process of acquiring Jnana—the direct realization of one's identity with Brahman. In this way, the Gita presents a holistic vision where action, devotion, and knowledge work together, leading the seeker toward liberation and the ultimate truth of existence.

When it comes to studying the Bhagavad Gita, people approach it in different ways, depending on their interest and ability. Most readers of the Bhagavad Gita fall into one of the following categories:

1. Casual Readers: Some people pick up a popular, often subsidized, copy of the Gita, perhaps handed to them or purchased at a railway station or airport. They might start reading on their own initiative, but many never make it past a few chapters.

2. Cherry-Picking Verses: Some readers cherry-pick key verses, treating them as standalone pieces of wisdom rather than engaging with the Gita as a complete work.

3. Memorization and Chanting: Others focus on reading, memorizing, or chanting the Sanskrit verses (parayana), engaging with the text on a more ritualistic or

devotional level.

4. Poetic Translations: There are readers who prefer poetized English versions of the Gita, often crafted by Western authors, who present the text in a way that's accessible and poetic.

5. Deep Analysis: Some individuals dive deeply into the text, studying one or two verses at a time with extensive analysis, commentary, and discussion. This approach, often done in classroom settings, can take several months to years.

Each of these approaches has its own merits, and people can benefit from the Gita in many ways. However, there is one approach that is less explored, which I believe holds unique value: reading the Bhagavad Gita as a complete seamless conversation between teacher and student, experiencing it in its entirety. This allows the reader to embark on the same transformative journey that Krishna and Arjuna undertook and get exposed to the wisdom of the text as a whole.

The purpose in writing another version of the Bhagavad Gita is to offer this experience—an accessible, clear, and concise version of the Gita that can be read in two hours, providing a deep and holistic understanding of its teachings in a single, transformative session. This, I believe, is a different kind of learning experience altogether for students of the Gita.

For me, the Gita is not just a collection of isolated insights or a text to be chanted—its way more than that- it's a powerful dialogue between teacher and student, a journey that takes Arjuna from despair to self-realization in one continuous flow. Reading the Gita as a whole uninterrupted conversation allows us to witness Arjuna's transformation—from a warrior unsure of his purpose to a seeker who finds his "why"—and to join Krishna, our own inner guide, on this journey. Experiencing this entire transformation in a seamless way is not just enlightening; but can be life-changing.

That's what drove me to to put together 'Shrimad Bhagavad Gita - A Seamless Reading' - the book that I never could quite find—a version that's clear, concise, and allows readers to fully immerse themselves in the conversation between Krishna and Arjuna. This book is intended to complement or enhance your existing learning setup, not to replace it.

In this book, I have endeavored to objectively evaluate which translations best convey the essence of the Gita, despite not being an expert in Sanskrit grammar or the various Upanishads. My aim is to present a version that stays true to the core teachings of the Gita, fully acknowledging that there are multiple schools of Vedanta with differing interpretations of its philosophical aspects. Since the Gita predates these schools, it is unlikely that Krishna or Sage Vyasa intended for it to be interpreted in multiple ways. The goal is to ensure that the integrity of the teaching is maintained across the entire text and its various parts.

I haven't numbered the verses as is commonly done in most versions, to facilitate a smooth reading experience. Instead, I've preserved the original flow and used paragraph breaks to indicate the separation of verses in the text. Anyone who wishes to reference the original verses can easily look them up in another book using this approach. Also, I have included the Bhagavad Gita verse references in brackets where necessary in the prologue.

It is essential to approach the Bhagavad Gita with an open mind, free from preconceived notions and distractions. The effort in this book is to provide a translation that is true to the text's essence, free of contradictions and ambiguities. The integrity of the teaching is paramount for me. My entire focus while learning the Gita from my teacher has been to avoid any inconsistencies. This commitment to clarity and coherence is reflected in this book, ensuring that you receive the teachings as authentically as possible.

Who is Shrimad Bhagavad Gita for?

The Bhagavad Gita is a text that speaks to anyone seeking deeper understanding, meaning, and direction in life. However, Krishna, in the Gita itself (BG 7.16), describes four types of people who approach him—people who could find the most value in the teachings. These are:

1. The Distressed (Arta): Those who turn to the divine in times of suffering or difficulty, seeking comfort and relief. They may be going through personal hardships, emotional turmoil, or existential crises. The Gita offers them solace and a path to peace by providing wisdom to rise above suffering.

2. The Seekers of Knowledge (Jijnasu): These are people who are naturally curious about the nature of life, the self, and the universe. They approach the Gita with a desire to understand deeper truths, seeking knowledge about existence, dharma, and spirituality.

3. The Seekers of Wealth (Artharthi): People who seek material or worldly gains might find value in the Gita by learning about right action, the pursuit of desires with integrity, and the importance of balancing spiritual and material aspirations. The Gita guides them toward success while maintaining a sense of detachment.

4. The Wise (Jnani): Those who already possess wisdom but continue to deepen their connection with the divine. For them, the Gita is a confirmation of their understanding and an advanced guide to realizing the highest truths.

For these individuals, there first has to be 'a need'—whether it's a longing for peace, knowledge, success, or truth. But beyond this need, there also needs to be 'a readiness to become a student'. The teachings of the Gita require more than intellectual engagement; they require the willingness to question, reflect, work and grow.

Arjuna, one of the central characters in the Gita, had known Krishna for a long time as a friend, but Krishna never imparted this profound knowledge to him before the battle of Kurukshetra. It wasn't because Krishna didn't want to, or because he was waiting for the war to begin. The reason was that Arjuna wasn't ready. It was only when Arjuna, overwhelmed by the moral and emotional conflict before the battle, submitted himself to Krishna as a student, sincerely asking for guidance in his best interest, that Krishna began his teaching. This moment of surrender and readiness is crucial; it highlights that true learning begins only when one is open and willing to receive.

Lastly, there must be 'an openness to listen with faith'. The Gita's wisdom cannot fully blossom in a closed heart. Faith in the process, in the message, and in the guidance of the teacher—whether that teacher is Krishna himself or a modern mentor—creates the openness needed for transformation.

The Bhagavad Gita is a timeless life manual that offers practical wisdom on living with purpose, navigating challenges, and finding inner peace. Anyone who feels the pull to seek, learn, or grow spiritually can benefit from reading the Bhagavad Gita, but the key lies in their readiness to listen, absorb, and transform its teachings into daily action.

A quick note on transliteration: Translating Sanskrit into English is no easy task, but to make the text more accessible to everyone, I've chosen a simple transliteration method that should help most readers pronounce the words fairly accurately. I also recognize that some Sanskrit terms don't have exact English equivalents. To bridge that gap, I've explained a few key terms at the outset in the prologue. Once you're familiar with these terms, you'll see them used directly in the translated text. This approach helps preserve the original meaning and integrity of the Gita's teachings.

I invite you to join me on this journey. To get the most out of this book, start by taking your time with the introductory pages—let the foundational concepts settle in. Then, when you're ready, set aside two hours on a weekend, find a quiet, distraction-free space, and immerse yourself in the Gita from Chapter 1 to Chapter 18.

The Srimad Bhagavad Gita is a perfect companion for both travel and your bedside table. You can make it a routine to read a chapter before bed, and perhaps even start your day with one. By doing so, you can go through the Gita three times a month! It also makes a thoughtful gift for someone who is open to its wisdom and can benefit from its teachings.

Krishna highlights the significance of this teaching with these words:

'Among all those who act according to My will, no one is dearer to Me than the one who shares this knowledge, and no one will ever be dearer on this earth.

Anyone who studies or recites this conversation of ours, which upholds righteousness, is performing a ritual of knowledge (Jnana Yajna), and through this, they are worshipping Me. This is My firm conviction.

Anyone who has faith in this teaching and does not criticize it, even if they simply listen to it, will be freed from the cycle of rebirth and attain the blessed realms of those who perform good deeds.'

Therefore, I encourage you to partake in this wisdom and share it with others as well.

The Gita is the essence, or "milk," of all the Upanishads, distilling their profound wisdom into a concise and accessible form. In the Bhagavad Gita, Krishna mentions, 'After many lifetimes, someone who truly understands that 'Vasudeva is everything' eventually finds their way to Me. Such a wise person is incredibly rare'. (7.19). Even a little progress on this path can save you from the greatest fears (2.40). If you have reached this point in your journey, you have already set foot on that path. I pray that you are blessed with the resolve and grace to become one of those rare individuals who attain true wisdom, finding peace, joy, and fulfillment in the knowledge of the Self. .

Acknowledgements

It is better to clarify at the outset that any mistakes in interpretation or limitations in understanding you may find are entirely my own, and not due to the teachers or institutions I've been associated with. This book has no affiliation with any person or organization and reflects my personal perspective and understanding of the subject.

I am deeply grateful to Swami Dayananda Saraswati of Arsha Vidya Gurukulam, whose translation of the Bhagavad Gita has been the most important resource in my work. Swami Dayananda Saraswati's magnum opus, the 9-volume, over 4000-page 'Bhagavad Gita Homestudy,' stands as the best resource for long-term study of the Bhagavad Gita. For those who are being introduced to the Bhagavad Gita for the first time, I strongly recommend his concise paperback, 'The Teaching of the Bhagavad Gita.'

Over the last two decades, many people from various organizations have helped keep the spark of spiritual seeking kindled in me. My journey with the Gita began at ISKCON in Belgaum in 2001, where I first encountered its teachings. From there, I traveled through the traditions of Madhva, Ramanuja, and Shankara. It wasn't until I reached the banks of the Ganga in 2011, during a motorcycle ride, and found Swami Sivananda's ashram, The Divine Life Society, that I developed a deep conviction in the teachings of the Gita. Swami Sivananda remains a real example of a realized Jnani, a Sthitaprajna as Krishna calls in the Gita. This experience sparked my quest for learning from a living guru, as tradition mandates.

I made a brief visit to the Chinmaya Mission in Pune before finding Swami Dayananda Saraswati of Arsha Vidya

Gurukulam, Coimbatore. There, I discovered my tradition, a sense of an old belonging and continue to recieve invaluable teachings from its Acharyas like Swami Paramarthananda, Swami Tattvavidananda, Swami Brahmavidananda, and Swamini Brahmaprajnanda. I am eternally grateful for all the coincidences, accidents, and deliberate encounters that have contributed to my spiritual growth. Without my teachers and fellow seekers, I would be nowhere. This has been the ecosystem that nourished and motivated me to embark on this book's journey. I still consider myself a student or sadhaka of Vedanta, a seeker on this path of wisdom, continually learning and growing in my understanding.

I am also thankful to my friends Mahesh, Girish, Janardhan, Rishikesh, Advait and Neha for, in their own ways, keeping me motivated on every project I undertake. I am also grateful to my parents, who have always respected and supported my views and preferences in spiritual matters. Lastly, I am grateful to my daughter Aanya, who gives me a meaningful reason to contribute—so that if not the world, she may benefit from my work.

Finally, I extend my gratitude to the Notion Press family for their support in publishing and distributing this book.

Prologue

The Bhagavad Gita is often viewed as a Hindu text, closely associated with the religious beliefs and practices of Hinduism. However, this perception can lead to misunderstandings that obscure its universal wisdom and timeless teachings. To grasp the true essence of the Gita, it's essential to approach it with an open mind, free from modern-day religious labels and assumptions. Here are some key points to consider before you embark on the study of the Bhagavad Gita:

The Gita Predates the Concept of Religious Identity

During the time of the Kurukshetra war in India, there was no concept of religious identity as we know it today. There were no Hindus, Muslims, Sikhs, Christians, or Jews. The word "Dharma" in the Gita does not refer to religion but to one's duty or obligations in life, based on one's stage in life (student, householder, retired, or monkhood). Understanding this distinction is crucial to appreciating the Gita's teachings beyond the confines of any specific religious doctrine.

The Bhagavad Gita emerged long before the practices of temple building and temple worship became common, which developed around the 4th to 6th century CE. While early Vedic traditions included forms of nature worship, the institutionalized temple rituals we see today came much later. The Gita, composed between 400 BCE and 200 CE, draws from the wisdom of the Upanishads, emphasizing devotion from the heart, selfless action, and the pursuit of knowledge. Its teachings go beyond rituals and formal practices, offering timeless guidance on how to live with purpose, faith, and understanding—wisdom that speaks to anyone, regardless of the era.

Although the Krishna of the Bhagavad Gita is worshipped as the same figure as the Krishna of folklore, we must be careful in our approach. In the Gita, Krishna serves as a spiritual guide, offering profound teachings on duty, self-realization, and the nature of reality to Arjuna on the battlefield. In contrast, the Krishna of folklore and the Bhagavata Purana is portrayed through stories of divine playfulness and miraculous feats. Krishna says in the Gita that he reveals himself to a person in the way they approach him. When studying the Gita, we first approach Krishna as Jagad Guru, the universal teacher, and then as the Paramatman, the Supreme Self.

The Gita Is a Moksha Shastra, Not a Religious Doctrine

In today's world, being religious or spiritual often means subscribing to a particular faith or religious organization, much like choosing a guided tour for a vacation. It's the easier path, where everything is curated for you—beliefs, rituals, and practices—all neatly packaged. However, much like the difference between a guided tour and an independent travel adventure, the spiritual journey offered by the Bhagavad Gita is vastly different from the modern-day religious experience.

When you plan your own travel, you immerse yourself in the local culture, navigate the challenges of foreign lands, and gain a firsthand experience of the world. Similarly, the Bhagavad Gita invites you to embark on a personal, unfiltered journey of self-discovery. It doesn't offer a pre-packaged spiritual experience but rather encourages you to explore, understand, and live its teachings in your own life.

Interestingly, the word "religion" comes from the Latin word 'religare', which means "to bind." The Bhagavad Gita, however, seeks to unbind us. It guides us on a journey of self-mastery, leading us towards an inquiry into the nature of our true self (atma vicharah). This journey ultimately leads to liberation or Moksha, the freedom from being a limited, incomplete, and wanting person.

The Gita's teachings are not about binding us to a set of beliefs or rituals but about freeing us—freeing our minds, intellect, and spirit. It is a Moksha Shastra, a science of freedom, guiding us towards our highest well-being and greatest accomplishment. The Bhagavad Gita is for everyone who seeks freedom from the cycle of Samsara—the endless loop of birth, suffering, death, and rebirth. Its message is timeless, universal, and above all, it is not a religion in the conventional sense. It is a path to true freedom, available to anyone who is willing to walk it.

Universal Teachings beyond Religious Boundaries

Most religions today are theocentric, centered around a deity with specific attributes, laws, and expectations. These religions often bind their followers to a set of beliefs and rituals, much like a travel agency binds you to a pre-planned itinerary. The Bhagavad Gita, however, presents a universal and individual-centered spiritual vision. It speaks directly to you, offering teachings that transcend any specific religion, tribe, caste, or race, while deeply rooted in a recognition of the divine in all aspects of life.

The Bhagavad Gita is a Moksha Shastra, a guide to liberation (Moksha) through the paths of Karma Yoga (the yoga of selfless action), Jnana Yoga (the yoga of knowledge), and Bhakti Yoga (the yoga of devotion). It is not merely a religious text meant to establish a new sect centered around Lord Krishna. The Vedas, including the Vedanta, focus on self-knowledge and realization rather than enforcing strict rituals or worshipping specific deities. Whether you see Krishna as a historical figure, an avatar of Vishnu, or as the Supreme Being, the teachings of the Gita are universal, timeless, and relevant to people from all backgrounds and walks of life.

The Gita's spirituality is taught as a practical and experiential path, offering universal principles that apply to everyone, regardless of their religious background. It teaches you to recognize the divine within yourself and understand what it truly means to be a whole being. While it does not rely on blind belief, it invites you to seek the divine presence within and around you, and to cultivate faith, devotion, and wisdom as pathways to inner freedom and peace.

The Teacher-Student Path in Vedanta

Before we begin to journey through this key Upanishad of the Gita, it's important to understand that learning Vedanta with the guidance of a teacher is crucial for truly grasping its wisdom. A teacher, or acharya, does more than just share knowledge—they help shape the student's understanding, leading them to a place of clarity. This is because a true acharya is deeply familiar with the shastram (scriptures) and rooted in truth. Their teachings resonate with logic and reason, encouraging the student to see things clearly rather than just accept things blindly. This kind of teaching not only builds trust but also helps students become emotionally independent.

In Vedanta, the teacher emphasizes atma-vichara—self-enquiry—as the path to liberation. Through self-enquiry, the student learns to differentiate between the true self (atma) and the non-self (anatma). Some might suggest that devotion (bhakti) or chanting (nama-sankirtanam) alone can lead to liberation, but without self-enquiry, it's incomplete.

A great example of this teacher-student relationship is in the Mahabharata, between Krishna and Arjuna. In the Bhagavad Gita, Krishna doesn't ask Arjuna to blindly follow him. Instead, he guides Arjuna step by step, helping him reason and reflect on his true duty (dharma) and the nature of the self. Krishna's approach is to lead Arjuna toward understanding through dialogue and self-reflection, showing the ideal role of a teacher.

A true acharya also never seeks personal glory. Like Krishna, they credit the lineage of teachers (parampara) and focus on the teachings themselves, putting the wisdom first. By teaching through both words and example, they guide the student toward self-realization and freedom.

Key Sanskrit Words to Know

Sanskrit is a rich and nuanced language, where a single word can hold multiple interpretations, depending on the context. The Gita was originally composed in this ancient language, and the precise choice of words by the sages is filled with intention. Before diving into the Bhagavad Gita, it's essential to grasp a few key Sanskrit words that frequently appear throughout the text. Words like Samsara,

Moha, Karma Moksha, Dharma, and Jnana are not just vocabulary—they are the pillars upon which the entire message of the Gita rests. Understanding these words can deepen your connection with the Gita's teachings, as each word carries layers of meaning that are often lost in translation.

Misinterpreting these can distort the teachings and lead to confusion, leaving you grappling with contradictions and disconnected from the profound wisdom the Gita offers. This is why Krishna himself emphasizes the importance of learning Self-knowledge from a knowledgeable and authentic teacher. The subtle nuances of these terms can't always be grasped through a casual reading or a quick internet search. Yet, today's spiritual landscape is crowded with various Gurus and communities, each offering their own take on ancient wisdom. While many of these sources can be enlightening, the risk is that in choosing what appeals to our tastes or social preferences, we might stray from the true essence of the teachings.

In this rush to find spiritual solutions, the ultimate goal—Truth—can sometimes get lost. Our longing for spiritual knowledge is genuine, but without careful discernment, we may find ourselves influenced by voices that lead us away from, rather than toward, the deeper understanding we seek. Therefore, approaching the Gita with the right guidance and a clear understanding of its key concepts is not just beneficial—it's essential.

Samsara

Krishna doesn't frequently use the term samsara in the Gita, although the concept is implied in several verses. The only instance where samsara is explicitly mentioned is in

Chapter 8, Verse 16.Samsara refers to the endless cycle of life, death, and rebirth—a continuous loop where we come into existence, live, die, and are born again. To picture it, think of a vast, turbulent ocean that every individual struggles to cross. The waves symbolize the never-ending cycle of birth and death, always pulling us back into worldly life.

Living in samsara means constantly taking on new bodies and going through the full range of human experiences: pleasure, pain, joy, sorrow, success, and failure. Each lifetime brings a new set of challenges and rewards, and we shift between different states of existence. Sometimes we may exist in higher, more pleasant realms (like svarga, or heavenly worlds), and at other times, in more difficult, painful ones (like naraka, or realms of suffering).

Samsara is often compared to a dream. Just as dreams are fleeting and not real, samsara is also temporary and ultimately an illusion. It is born from ignorance, from mistakenly identifying the changing aspects of life—like our body, mind, and emotions—as our true identity. This confusion leads us to feel separate from the ultimate reality, which is the oneness of all existence (Ishvara, or supreme consciousness).

Breaking free from this cycle and reaching moksha (liberation) requires us to first realize we are caught in samsara. Recognizing that we are part of this cycle is the crucial first step toward liberation. Only by understanding that samsara is not the ultimate truth can we start the journey toward discovering our real nature and escaping the cycle of rebirth.

In the Bhagavad Gita, Arjuna's crisis on the battlefield represents the experience of Samsara. His despair and confusion mirror the inner struggle everyone faces in trying to navigate the cycle of existence. His inner conflict sets the stage for the teachings that follow, which provide a path to transcend Samsara and achieve true freedom.

Yet, it is not just the cycle of birth and death that binds us, but also the delusion that obscures our vision—Mohah. While Samsara is the external cycle we are caught in, Mohah is the internal confusion that keeps us entangled in that cycle. Without clarity, we mistake the temporary for the eternal and get lost in the struggle between right and wrong, truth and illusion.

Mohah

Mohah can be understood as a state of deep confusion, where we lose sight of what really matters and can no longer distinguish between what's real and what's false. It clouds our judgment, making it hard to see the difference between our true self (atma) and everything that isn't—like the body, mind, or possessions (anatma). It also confuses our sense of what's right (dharma) and what's wrong (adharma), leading us to make poor choices.

This kind of confusion comes from ignorance (avidya), and it keeps us stuck in a cycle of misunderstanding and suffering. When we're trapped in moha, we lose our sense of right and wrong, and this often leads us to neglect our responsibilities. The poor decisions we make under moha result in wrongdoing (papam), which brings grief (shokah). This grief, in turn, keeps us trapped in the endless cycle of struggle and rebirth, known as samsara.

In the Bhagavad Gita, Arjuna experiences Mohah when he stands on the battlefield, facing the prospect of fighting his own family and friends. Overwhelmed with sorrow and confusion, he questions whether the battle is even righteous and loses sight of his duty as a warrior. This confusion, driven by mohah, paralyzes him, leaving him unable to act until Krishna steps in to guide him. Through Krishna's wisdom, Arjuna is able to see through his delusion and reclaim his purpose.

To make this more relatable, think of a child sucking their thumb, mistaking their own saliva for their mother's milk. No matter how much they suck, they will never be satisfied. In the same way, we often chase temporary pleasures or worldly achievements, thinking they will bring lasting happiness. But just like the child with their thumb, we end up unfulfilled, and our confusion only deepens.

Mohah, or deep confusion, blinds us to our true nature and distorts our sense of right and wrong, leading us into a cycle of poor decisions and suffering. This confusion stems from Maya, the cosmic illusion that clouds our perception of reality. Maya distorts how we experience life by influencing us through the three fundamental qualities, or Gunas—Sattva, Rajas, and Tamas.

Maya and the Gunas

Maya is often explained as an illusion or veil that distorts our perception of reality, leading us to misunderstand our true nature. Imagine it as wearing tinted glasses that alter the way everything looks. In Vedanta, Maya creates this illusion through three primary powers known as the Gunas.

The Gunas—Sattva, Rajas, and Tamas—are the building blocks of how we experience life under Maya's influence:

Sattva (clarity and wisdom) is associated with jnana-shakti (the power of knowledge). When Sattva predominates, we experience peace, clarity, and understanding. However, this clarity can also lead to attachment to positive experiences, creating a dependency on them.

Rajas (activity and desire) is linked to kriya-shakti (the power of action). It drives us to act, desire, and be constantly active. While Rajas generates energy and ambition, it also leads to restlessness and a preoccupation with the results of our actions, fostering dissatisfaction and continuous striving.

Tamas (inertia and ignorance) corresponds to dravya-shakti (the power of inertia). Tamas creates a sense of heaviness, lethargy, and confusion. When Tamas is dominant, it results in delusion, indifference, and inaction, obstructing personal growth and understanding.

These Gunas interact in various proportions, shaping how we perceive the world and ourselves. For example, under the influence of Rajas, one might identify strongly with their constant activity. Under Tamas, one might mistake lethargy or confusion as inherent traits. This misidentification is a way Maya keeps us bound.

Krishna provides a comprehensive understanding of these Gunas in Chapter 14 of the Bhagavad Gita, titled 'Guna-traya-Vibhaga Yoga' (The Division of the Three Gunas). He explains that the Gunas—Sattva, Rajas, and Tamas—bind us to the cycle of birth and rebirth. By transcending these Gunas, one can achieve Moksha (liberation).

The ultimate goal is to rise above the influence of these Gunas, reaching a state known as Gunatita, where one is free from the fluctuations of clarity, restlessness, and inertia. By understanding the interplay of Maya and the Gunas, we gain insight into the nature of our perception and the path to true self-realization.

Dharma

Dharma is a word that doesn't have a direct equivalent in European languages. It is often mistakenly interpreted as religion by many translators. However, dharma is not a religion in the conventional sense. While it encompasses ethical principles and duties, it is not tied to any specific religious doctrine or belief system. Instead, it encompasses a wide range of meanings, all centered around a core idea.

At its core, dharma means "that which upholds." It represents the universal laws, moral order, and ethical duties that maintain harmony and balance in the world. It's the guiding principles that keep everything running smoothly, both in the natural world and in our personal lives. By following your dharma—whether it's fulfilling your responsibilities, being honest in your relationships, or helping others—you contribute to the overall harmony of the universe. Thats the idea.

Dharma is closely related to karma—the law of cause and effect. Acting in accordance with dharma generates positive outcomes, both materially and spiritually, believed to be creating what is known as punyam (spiritual merit). This merit enriches your life and supports your spiritual growth. Essentially, doing good attracts good back into your life. Even if dharma is challenged or distorted, it will eventually reassert itself because it forms the foundation of everything.

When you act according to dharma, you help uphold these principles and prevent them from falling into disuse. In return, dharma helps protect you from falling into adharma (unrighteousness). This protection is not just about avoiding negative outcomes; it's about maintaining balance and integrity in your life. The idea that "what goes around comes around" perfectly captures this principle. By acting with righteousness and fulfilling your duties, the positive effects of your actions often come back to benefit you. However, following dharma offers relative protection—it helps maintain balance and harmony in your life. However, ultimate protection and liberation come from jnanam (knowledge of the true self). While dharma guides your actions and keeps you in alignment with universal principles, true liberation or freedom (moksha) is only possible through the realization of your true self, which is achieved through jnanam. Without this deeper understanding, you may live a righteous life but still be bound by ignorance and the cycle of birth and death.

In many contexts, dharma can be understood as universal ethics which includes universal values and principles that apply to everyone regardless of time, religion, gender, age, race, country, or social status. Examples of this include: Ahimsa (Non-hurting or harmlessness), Satyam (Truthfulness), Asteyam (Non-stealing), Shaucham (Cleanliness), Indriya-nigraha (Restraint of the senses)

These values are considered ethical and moral imperatives that everyone should follow, reflecting universal principles of right conduct. In contrast to this, there could be individual ethics or duties that are specifically applicable to an individual's unique context or situation. This involves correctly interpreting and applying universal dharma in particular contexts. For example, while non-hurting (ahimsa) is a universal principle, how it is applied can vary depending on specific circumstances and one's role in life. This helps individuals understand and fulfill their duties accurately in their particular situation.

Krishna elaborates on the concept of dharma for individuals throughout the Bhagavad Gita. This exploration will provide a deeper understanding of how dharma applies personally and universally. While Dharma guides us toward righteous living by aligning our actions with universal principles, it is Karma—the law of action and its consequences—that determines the outcome of those actions. The interplay between Dharma and Karma shapes not only our present life but also the cycle of birth and rebirth, making every choice we make profoundly significant.

Karma

Karma is all about action—what we do and the choices we make. But it's not just about the act itself; it's also about the ripple effect that follows. Every action we take has consequences, and these consequences shape our lives and the cycle of birth and rebirth (samsara). It's like a chain reaction that keeps life moving forward.

When we act out of personal desires, like wanting something really badly or avoiding something we fear (raga-dvesha), without thinking about what's right or fair (dharma), our actions tie us down. It's like carrying the weight of our choices, and that weight keeps us stuck. But when we do things with a sense of duty, without expecting anything in return, our actions don't have that same heavy baggage.

The most meaningful kind of karma is when we do things not for ourselves but to clear our mind, making it more peaceful and focused. This is where karma becomes karma yoga—a way of turning our everyday actions into a spiritual practice. Instead of getting caught up in what we want or don't want, we learn to act with a bigger purpose in mind.

In the Bhagavad Gita, Krishna talks a lot about how we can transform our everyday actions into something deeper, turning them into karma yoga. He explains how, by changing the way we approach life, we can make our actions a path to freedom. You'll see this idea come up again and again as you explore the Gita further.

Here's the key: no matter how much we do, karma alone can't give us the kind of lasting freedom or peace we're all looking for (moksha). Our actions can help prepare us, like clearing the way, but it's understanding our true nature that sets us free. Imagine you're a kid who's already wealthy but doesn't know it. You don't have to work hard to become rich—you already are. In the same way, our real self (atman) is already free. It's just a matter of realizing it.

Yoga

Yoga, derived from the Sanskrit root "Yuj," meaning "to join" or "to unite," refers to the practice of connecting with the ultimate reality, whether understood as Consciousness, God, or Oneness. The essence of Yoga is to transcend our current ways of thinking, behaving, and choosing, and to bring about a profound change in our perception, attitude, and behavior. It involves sensitizing ourselves to recognize the higher reality that underlies our existence, which is subtle yet all-encompassing, and serves as the ultimate truth, freedom, and harmony within us.

In the Bhagavad Gita, 'Yoga' refers to the path that leads to Moksha, or liberation, and each chapter covers a different aspect or stage of this journey. That's why every chapter title ends with 'Yogah' indicating which part of the spiritual path is being discussed.

For example, in 'Arjuna Vishada Yogah' (Arjuna's Despair), you might wonder, how can Arjuna's despair be called 'Yoga'? The idea is that even Arjuna's despair is a crucial stage or aspect of his path to spiritual growth. His inner turmoil, confusion, and struggle are part of his personal Yoga—his process of moving toward self-realization. The same applies to 'Bhakti Yogah' (the Yoga of devotion). Here, the devotional aspect of Yoga is explored, showing how sincere devotion and surrender are also essential stages on the path to spiritual growth. Each chapter highlights different parts of this broader journey, emphasizing various aspects of Yoga.

Having said that, overall Yoga can be understood in two primary contexts: as a discipline (Karma Yoga) and as the pursuit of knowledge (Jnana Yoga or Sankhya Yoga).

In the context of discipline, Karma Yoga refers to performing actions with the proper attitude aligned with universal values, without attachment to the results. At the heart of Karma Yoga is the attitude of Ishwararpana Buddhi—offering all your actions to Ishwara or God or the divine and seeing yourself as a tool in the divine plan. Alongside this is Prasada Buddhi—accepting the outcomes of your actions, whatever they may be, with gratitude, like receiving prasada (a sacred offering). Karma Yoga transforms ordinary actions and work into worship, and life into a spiritual journey.

Practicing Karma Yoga helps to purify the mind by reducing selfishness and cultivating humility and devotion. It brings inner freedom by breaking the cycle of worry, fear, and frustration over results. This, in turn, prepares you for deeper spiritual practices like meditation and self-inquiry, making Karma Yoga a stepping stone to greater wisdom and peace. Karma Yoga prepares the mind for self-knowledge, which leads to Moksha, or liberation. Krishna describes Yoga as "yogah karmasu kaushalam," meaning that Yoga is the skill in action. This skill, or kaushalam, is the ability to interpret situations and make decisions effectively according to dharma (the right thing to do). An adept practitioner of Karma Yoga, called Yogarudha, is disciplined and prepared for spiritual pursuit.

Preparatory disciplines are varied and tailored to individual needs. These include ethical living (dharma), and specific practices like Hatha Yoga (which involves physical exercises and breathing techniques), Bhakti Yoga (the path of devotion), or Upasana (meditation). These practices assist in the spiritual journey but are not strictly categorized under Karma Yoga.

Once the mind is prepared through Karma Yoga, the pursuit of wisdom, or Jnana Yoga, begins. This path involves three steps: Shravanam (listening to the teachings from a teacher), Mananam (reflecting and removing doubts), and Nididhyasanam (meditating on the true nature of the self). This path leads to the knowledge of Atma (the true self), which is essential for Moksha.

Sankhya Yoga in the Bhagavad Gita refers to the discriminative inquiry into the nature of the self and reality, focusing on the distinction between the eternal self (Purusha) and the material world (Prakriti). It provides the intellectual framework that prepares the mind for Jnana Yoga, where the realization of the self brings freedom from existential and emotional sorrow.

Krishna describes in great detail these two Yogas in the Bhagavad Gita—Karma Yoga as the preparatory path and Jnana Yoga as the path to self-realization, leading to

Moksha.

Let us now turn our attention to Shreyas, the ultimate good or highest goal of life. While Yoga provides the methods and practices to refine our actions and understanding, Shreyas represents the pursuit of the highest good and true fulfillment in life, attained through self-realization and liberation.

Shreyas

In the Bhagavad Gita, Arjuna asks Krishna about Shreyas, the highest good, rather than just inquiring about the right or best actions to take. This question goes beyond mere decisions and actions; it seeks to understand the ultimate purpose and true fulfillment in life. Shreyas is about achieving the highest or absolute good, which is even greater than concepts of right and wrong. It represents the knowledge that leads to liberation, or freedom from all forms of unhappiness.

On the other hand, Preyas refers to immediate pleasures and is linked with a lack of discernment. While Shreyas is associated with wisdom and the path of knowledge, Preyas offers only temporary satisfaction. You can't follow both paths at the same time; you must choose one.

Shreyas is essentially the path of knowledge (5.5), the best way to achieve ultimate freedom and peace. Arjuna's question about shreyas reflects a deeper quest for lasting truth and fulfillment, aiming for the highest good that goes beyond everyday concerns.

Moksha

Simply put moksha means freedom from limitation. Think of everything that makes us feel we are a limited, inadequate, incomplete, wanting, lacking, desiring person. This everything is our ignorance or misunderstanding or misconception. And it mainly arises from our identification with this body-sense-mind complex that we think we are. The only thing that can free us from this ignorance is the right understanding, right self-knowledge.

The freedom from this ignorance-born erroneous identification with the body and mind is moksha. Moksha is freedom from emotional dependence; freedom from being a wanting person. That's why Moksha is also known as parama-shreyah or one's greatest state of wellness.

Moksha is freedom from samsara, the beginningless, endless cycle of births and deaths. It is freedom from self-ignorance and misperception of both oneself and the world. These misperceptions result in misconceptions that often evoke misplaced emotional responses in the form of unease or distress (including jealousy, anger, depression, fear, anxiety, regret, etc.) too often resulting in inappropriate action and sorrow. All such unfortunate responses leave a residue of unfinished business that perpetuates the cycle of emotionally driven problems known as samsara, a cycle that is never-ending until broken by correct knowledge and understanding of oneself and the world.

Moksha is not an achievement or a process of becoming something new; it is the realization of the freedom that is already within us. This freedom is obscured by ignorance, and self-knowledge is about recognizing and owning this inherent freedom. Moksha is simply the uncovering of our true nature, which is always present but needs to be realized. It is not an event or a future attainment but the recognition of our ever-existing essential nature. All spiritual efforts aim to reveal and embrace this true nature fully.

In the Bhagavad Gita, the path to Moksha is essentially about self-knowledge or Atma-jnanam, which is the realization of one's true self. Krishna presents this profound knowledge to Arjuna in the 2nd chapter, but simply providing this knowledge isn't enough. The key challenge is that an unprepared mind can't truly assimilate and understand Atma-jnanam

To prepare for this realization, various disciplines and practices are emphasized. Karma yoga, for instance, cultivates ethical behavior and emotional resilience, helping one navigate life's ups and downs while fostering emotional intelligence. It also includes bhakti, or reverence, towards existence, nature, fellow beings, and the divine within us all. Other practices detailed in the Gita, such as yama (prohibitions), niyama (injunctions), asanam (postures), pranayama (breathing exercises), pratyahara (sense control), and dharana (concentration), are essential for disciplining the body and mind. These practices help remove mental impurities like restlessness and agitation, paving the way for deeper meditation (dhyana), which focuses the mind and helps contemplate the truth of Atma.

Krishna's teaching is not about choosing from a variety of yogas; rather, it's about gradually moving closer to divinity, truth and freedom. The journey of spirituality involves turning this knowledge into deep, lived understanding. This comprehensive approach helps one move from intellectual knowledge to true realization of the self, which is the essence of achieving Moksha.

In the Bhagavad Gita, Arjuna's inquiry about Shreyas reflects a profound quest for understanding the ultimate good that transcends ordinary decisions and actions. Shreyas is about pursuing the highest good, which aligns with achieving true fulfillment and liberation.

As we move from the concept of Shreyas to Moksha, we see that Moksha is the ultimate realization of this highest good. It represents the ultimate state of well-being and liberation from the cycle of rebirth and emotional distress. This freedom is not an achievement but a recognition of our inherent, ever-present true nature. Understanding Moksha requires embracing the realization that the freedom we seek is already within us, uncovered through the right knowledge and self-awareness.

Jnanam & Vijnanam

In the Bhagavad Gita, jnanam and vijnanam are two key aspects of spiritual wisdom that guide the seeker towards liberation. Jnanam refers to intellectual or theoretical knowledge, particularly the understanding of the true nature of the self (atman), the universe, and the divine (Brahman). This concept is central to Vedanta and runs throughout the Gita as Krishna repeatedly emphasizes the importance of self-knowledge for spiritual progress. Jnanam, in this sense, is not merely academic learning but the deep, clear understanding that dispels ignorance (avidya)—the root cause of human suffering.

In contrast, vijnanam represents experiential wisdom, the lived and direct realization of the truths understood through jnanam. While jnanam gives the seeker clarity about reality, such as the eternal nature of the self beyond the body and mind, vijnanam is the full assimilation of this knowledge into one's being, enabling the person to live in harmony with these truths. It moves beyond intellectual grasp to become a transformative experience that manifests in detachment, equanimity, and self-mastery.

The Gita weaves these concepts through various chapters, urging the seeker to first acquire jnanam by studying the nature of the self and the universe, and then embody that knowledge through practice, leading to vijnanam. The culmination of this process is moksha—liberation from the cycle of birth and death. Krishna's teachings in the Gita present jnanam as the foundation for spiritual wisdom, while vijnanam is the actual realization of that wisdom, ultimately guiding the seeker to self-realization and unity with the divine.

Sankhya Yoga

Sankhya Yoga, as presented in the second chapter of the Bhagavad Gita, refers to the path of knowledge through systematic and discriminating inquiry. While the term Sankhya also refers to the philosophy founded by the sage Kapila, which emphasizes a dualistic view of Purusha (consciousness) and Prakriti (matter), in the Gita, Sankhya Yoga is more closely aligned with Jnana Yoga, focusing on the intellectual understanding of the eternal self.

In this context, Jnana (self-knowledge) is not merely intellectual, but leads to a deeper understanding of who we truly are, beyond the physical body and mind. The focus in Sankhya Yoga is on recognizing the distinction between the eternal self (Purusha) and the material world (Prakriti). Through this understanding, one can realize that liberation comes from discerning the unchanging reality within us, distinct from the changing phenomena of the material world.

Though Kapila's Sankhya system does not involve a Supreme Deity (Ishvara), the Bhagavad Gita incorporates the concept of Ishvara, integrating the analytical approach of Sankhya with the practical paths of Karma Yoga and Bhakti Yoga. Sankhya Yoga in the Gita represents the knowledge needed to walk the spiritual path toward self-realization and inner freedom.

Thus, Sankhya Yoga serves as a guide to self-reflection, helping one discern what is permanent and unchanging from the impermanent aspects of life. It encourages clarity of mind and self-awareness, essential for achieving inner peace and purpose.

Jnana Yoga

Jnana Yoga is the path of knowledge leading to liberation (moksha). Also known as Jnana Marga or the "path of knowledge," it involves seeking understanding of the Self (Atma) and the ultimate reality (Brahman). This path includes studying scriptures, learning from a teacher, contemplation, and meditation to achieve self-realization and a true understanding of one's nature.

A related term, Jnana-nishtha, signifies unwavering steadiness in the realization of Brahman. It represents a state where the understanding of the Self as limitless and whole remains constant. Achieving Jnana-nishtha requires not just learning, but deep internalization of the truth, involving vairagya (dispassion) and a consistent acceptance of Brahman as the ultimate reality, free from doubt.

Jnana itself refers to clear, doubt-free knowledge that reveals the essence of reality and oneself. It is not an addition but the very essence that uncovers what is already present, essential for achieving liberation by dispelling ignorance and false beliefs.

Sankhya provides a philosophical framework that explains the distinction between the eternal self (Purusha) and the material world (Prakriti). Though discussed in the second chapter of the Bhagavad Gita, it is not a direct path to self-realization like Jnana Yoga but offers a systematic analysis of reality. Sankhya's teachings can complement Jnana Yoga by offering conceptual clarity, but it is more a background philosophy than a practical discipline.

Jnana Yoga integrates elements of Karma Yoga (the yoga of selfless action). Krishna emphasizes that integrating knowledge with action is crucial for liberation. In Chapter 3, Krishna teaches that performing one's duties selflessly purifies the mind, preparing it for self-knowledge. Karma Yoga helps dissolve the ego and fosters equanimity, essential for Jnana.

In Chapter 5, Verse 4, Krishna unifies the paths:

"While those who lack understanding might argue that Sankhya and Karma Yoga are separate paths, the truth is that someone who genuinely practices even one of these paths will experience the benefits of both."

Here, Krishna shows that selfless action paves the way towards discriminative knowledge, or they complement each other. Karma Yoga purifies the mind, while Jnana Yoga provides the experiential understanding needed to realize the self, leading to liberation.

The process of attaining Jnana Yoga involves three main stages: Shravanam, listening to teachings from a qualified teacher to remove doubts about reality; Mananam, reflecting deeply on these teachings to resolve contradictions; and Nididhyasana, continuous meditation on the truth, resolving wrong ideas and habitual misidentifications.

Jnana Yoga requires a life dedicated to understanding the true self, preparing through Karma Yoga, and developing vairagya to detach from worldly desires and focus on self-realization.

Bhakti Yoga

Transitioning from Jnana Yoga, we now explore Bhakti Yoga, which is a deeply personal and heartfelt devotion to the divine. Unlike the intellectual inquiry of Jnana or the discriminative analysis of Sankhya, Bhakti focuses on cultivating a profound emotional and spiritual connection with Ishvara (the divine). It's more than just feelings; it's a commitment that shapes our daily actions and choices.

At its core, Bhakti blends devotion, love, respect, and trust, acknowledging the divine presence in all aspects of life. This devotion is expressed through our actions, seamlessly integrating with Karma Yoga, the path of selfless action. In Bhakti, every action becomes an offering to Ishvara, transforming daily tasks into acts of worship. Bhakti intertwines with our commitment to dharma, the moral duty of doing what is right and just. Through love of dharma, we naturally develop a deeper love for Ishvara.

The highest form of Bhakti, known as para-bhakti, involves complete surrender to the divine—a state where the devotee feels a deep sense of oneness with God. This practice helps us recognize the divine presence in all aspects of life, not through intellectual self-enquiry but through devotional surrender. Bhakti teaches us to dedicate all our actions in service of the divine, performing our duties with love and reverence.

While rituals such as singing, dancing, and chanting are important expressions of devotion, Bhakti Yoga is much deeper than these outward acts. As highlighted in the Bhagavad Gita, true Bhakti is the devotion of the heart, a state of unwavering love, surrender, and commitment to the divine.

Dhyana Yoga

Meditation, or dhyana, is the practice of focusing your mind on one specific thing—a thought, object, or form. It's about fully concentrating while gently letting go of all other distractions. For a student of Vedanta, though, meditation is more than just a practice you do once in a while- it is a powerful discipline for personal and spiritual growth. Eventually, the meditation practice becomes a mindset that shapes how you see the world throughout your day. The way you practice meditation depends on where you are in your spiritual journey.

In karma yoga (the path of selfless action), meditation helps calm and purify the mind. The goal isn't immediate enlightenment but to prepare the mind by letting go of attachment to the outcomes of your actions. When you meditate on a form of the divine, called saguna-brahma (the divine with attributes), there is a sense of separation between you and what you're meditating on. This practice, known as saguna-brahma-upasanam, brings peace of mind and prepares you to absorb atma-jnana (self-knowledge). In this kind of meditation, you start by seeing everything as a reflection of the divine (Bhagavan). Over time, as your understanding deepens, you realize that everything is not just a reflection—it is the divine itself.

In jnana yoga (the path of knowledge), meditation is used for self-inquiry. It helps you understand that your true self is not separate from Brahman (the universal consciousness). Here, meditation is about realizing your true nature, not about doing something specific. When meditation focuses on discovering who you are—beyond your body and mind—it's called nididhyasanam or nirguna-brahma-upasanam (meditation on the formless divine). In this deeper form of meditation, the line between you and the object of meditation fades, and you directly experience your true self.

It's important to know that dhyana (meditation) or dhyana yoga is not a separate path by itself. Both types of meditation—whether in karma yoga or jnana yoga—are valuable disciplines for spiritual growth. While their approaches may differ, both lead toward the same goal: freedom, or moksha (liberation). In the Bhagavad Gita, Krishna emphasizes the importance of meditation, especially in Chapter 6, where he explains how it helps you connect with your deeper self and discover your true nature.

Yajna

In the Bhagavad Gita, yajna represents a form of worship and devotion to the divine or Ishwara, originally practiced through fire rituals and offerings. More than just a ritual, it's a way of prayerfully connecting with the divine, seeking grace to clear obstacles caused by past actions (karma). This grace helps a person fully realize the knowledge they've gained through spiritual learning.

A traditional yajna involves five key elements: the person performing the ritual (yajamana), their spouse, the sacred fire, the chanting of mantras, and offerings. While these rituals are meaningful, the Gita teaches that no action bound by time, no matter how well performed, can bring about the timeless result of ultimate freedom, or moksha. This is because the infinite cannot be achieved through limited actions.

However, the idea of yajna extends beyond rituals. It can also be a way of living, where every action becomes an offering to the divine. This is known as karma yoga, where a person performs all actions selflessly and with devotion to the divine or Ishwara, freeing themselves from the consequences of their actions. Additionally, sharing knowledge can be seen as a form of yajna—a 'sacrifice of wisdom' which is equally important on the path to spiritual growth.

As you begin reading the Gita, keep these Sanskrit words in mind—they will help you truly grasp its deeper, universal message.

The Names of Krishna and Arjuna

In Sanskrit literature, it is common for individuals to be referred to by various names or epithets, each reflecting different aspects of their personality, deeds, lineage, or divine nature. These names are not merely labels but encapsulate deep symbolic meanings and stories that often connect to the broader cultural and spiritual heritage found in texts like the Mahabharata and Vedas.

In the Bhagavad Gita, the conversation between Krishna and Arjuna is rich with such names, and understanding these names adds depth to their dialogue. Each name serves as a reminder of the broader context of the epic and the roles these characters play in the cosmic drama. I wanted to introduce these names at the beginning of the book so that as you read the Bhagavad Gita, you can easily recognize and connect with the Sanskrit names without needing repeated explanations. This approach allows us to stay immersed in the flow of the conversation between Krishna and Arjuna, making the experience more seamless and engaging. Now, let's explore each of these names together.

Names of Arjuna

Partha: Arjuna is often referred to as 'Partha,' meaning 'son of Pritha' (another name for Kunti, his mother). This name highlights his royal lineage and his connection to the noble Kuru dynasty. Kunti was known for her wisdom and devotion, and by calling Arjuna 'Partha,' Krishna reminds him of his heritage and the responsibility that comes with it.

Gudakesha: 'Gudakesha' means 'conqueror of sleep,' a name that reflects Arjuna's discipline and focus. In the Mahabharata, Arjuna was known for his relentless practice and commitment, often engaging in meditation and archery even at night. This name signifies his determination and ability to overcome distractions.

Dhananjaya: 'Dhananjaya' means 'winner of wealth.' Arjuna earned this title during the Rajasuya Yajna, when he conquered many kings and brought immense wealth to his brother Yudhishthira for the great sacrifice. The name symbolizes his prowess and success in battle, as well as his role as a provider for his family and kingdom.

Kaunteya: Another name derived from his mother, Kunti, 'Kaunteya' emphasizes his maternal lineage. It reflects the affection and pride his family has in him, as well as the virtues he has inherited from his mother, who was known for her unwavering faith and resilience.

Kiritin: 'Kiritin' means 'one who wears a crown.' This name is a reminder of Arjuna's royal status and his responsibilities as a prince. In the Mahabharata, Arjuna receives a divine diadem from the gods, symbolizing his destined role as a great warrior and leader.

Bharatarshabha: Meaning 'best of the Bharatas,' this name emphasizes Arjuna's status as a great warrior and a distinguished member of the Kuru dynasty, descendants of King Bharata.

Bharatashreshtha: Similar to the name above, it translates to 'the greatest among the Bharatas' or 'the most distinguished of the Bharata dynasty.'

Anagha: This name means 'sinless' or 'faultless,' highlighting Arjuna's pure heart and virtuous character, which make him worthy of receiving Krishna's divine guidance.

Pandava: Referring to Arjuna as the 'son of Pandu,' this name connects him to his father's legacy and his duty as one of the Pandavas, the righteous princes of the Mahabharata.

Savyasachi: This name means 'ambidextrous,' showcasing Arjuna's exceptional skill in wielding weapons with both hands, making him a formidable warrior on the battlefield.

Vijaya: Meaning 'victorious,' this name reflects Arjuna's invincible nature in battle, symbolizing his destiny to triumph in the righteous war.

Names of Krishna

Madhava: 'Madhava' is one of Krishna's names, meaning 'husband of Lakshmi' or 'descendant of the Madhu clan.' This name connects Krishna to the goddess of wealth,

Lakshmi, and signifies his role as the divine sustainer and protector of the world. It also links him to his Yadava lineage, reflecting his royal birth and divine origin.

Govinda: 'Govinda' means 'protector of cows' or 'one who brings pleasure to the senses.' This name refers to Krishna's early life as a cowherd in Vrindavan, where he was beloved by all for his playful and loving nature. It also signifies his role as a protector and caretaker of all beings, symbolizing his compassion and devotion to the welfare of his devotees.

Hrishikesha: 'Hrishikesha' means 'lord of the senses.' This name highlights Krishna's mastery over the senses and his ability to control and direct them. In the Bhagavad Gita, Krishna often guides Arjuna to control his mind and senses, leading him on the path of righteousness. The name underscores Krishna's divine wisdom and his role as a spiritual guide.

Janardana: 'Janardana' means 'one who agitates or moves people' or 'one who is worshiped by people.' Krishna, as Janardana, is the one who stirs people to action and devotion. This name reflects his role as a guide and protector, leading people towards their destiny and helping them fulfill their duties.

Vasudeva: 'Vasudeva' refers to Krishna as the son of Vasudeva, his father. This name emphasizes his human birth and his role as a divine incarnation in the mortal world. It also highlights the dual nature of Krishna as both a human prince and a divine being, bridging the gap between the earthly and the divine.

Keshava: 'Keshava' refers to Krishna as the slayer of the demon Keshi, symbolizing his role as the divine protector who destroys evil and upholds righteousness.

Achyuta: This name means 'infallible' or 'unchanging,' highlighting Krishna's divine nature as the eternal, unchanging truth, who remains steady and reliable in all circumstances.

Yogeshvara: 'Yogeshvara' means 'lord of yoga,' emphasizing Krishna's mastery over spiritual knowledge and his ability to guide others on the path of yoga, or union with the divine.

Madhusudana: This name means 'slayer of the demon Madhu,' reflecting Krishna's role as a destroyer of evil forces and a protector of dharma (righteousness).

Varshneya: Referring to Krishna as a descendant of the Vrishni clan, this name emphasizes his royal lineage and his connection to the Yadava dynasty.

Purushottama: Refers to Lord Krishna as the Supreme Being who transcends both the perishable material world and the imperishable soul. This name highlights Krishna's role as the highest divine being, the source of all creation, and the final goal of spiritual pursuit.

As Krishna and Arjuna address each other with these names, they are not just speaking to one another as individuals but invoking the broader spiritual and cultural narratives that they embody. Understanding these names enriches the reading of the Bhagavad Gita, offering insights into the characters' identities and the spiritual teachings conveyed in their dialogue.

Shrimad Bhagavad Gita is a Pramana

The Shrimad Bhagavad Gita is a profound spiritual dialogue between a student, Arjuna, and his teacher, Krishna, woven into beautiful poetry. It mirrors our own struggles and dilemmas, and as we follow Arjuna's journey from confusion to clarity, we find our own paths illuminated. The Gita is a guide to living a life of peace, freedom, and love. Embracing its teachings can lead to a happy and meaningful life.

The Bhagavad Gita is not just a sacred text; it is also a Pramana, a trusted means of knowledge. It goes beyond what we can see or infer and directly reveals truths about the self and the nature of reality. For instance, Krishna teaches Arjuna that he is not the body or mind, but the eternal Atma—an insight that cannot be grasped through the senses or ordinary logic. This shift in perspective requires guidance from a reliable source, and the Gita, as a Pramana, plays that crucial role, helping us move from ignorance to self-awareness.

The Gita also provides practical wisdom for everyday life. Krishna's teachings on karma yoga, the path of selfless action and devotion, show that by acting without attachment to outcomes, we can purify our minds and prepare them for deeper self-knowledge. These teachings have stood the test of time and have guided countless seekers over the centuries, proving the Gita's reliability as a Pramana for understanding the self and finding purpose.

Because of its blend of profound spiritual insights and practical guidance, the Gita is often the first text recommended for students of Vedanta. It sets a strong foundation for deeper study of the Upanishads and other Vedantic texts, making it a perfect starting point for anyone on a journey of self-discovery. Join me on this journey of reflection and understanding, as the timeless wisdom of the Gita leads us towards a life of joy, freedom, and fulfillment.

CHAPTER ONE

The Despair of Arjuna

Arjuna-Vishada Yogah

Dhritarashtra asked:

Sanjaya, gathered on the sacred battlefield of Kurukshetra, what did my sons and the Pandavas, eager to fight, do?

Sanjaya narrated:

As King Duryodhana observed the Pandavas' army arranged for battle, he approached his teacher, Drona, and began to speak.

O Teacher, please take a moment to observe this mighty army assembled by the sons of Pandu. It's led by your brilliant disciple, Dhrishtadyumna, the son of Drupada.

Here stand unmatched warriors, akin to Bhima and Arjuna in battle, each a master archer in their own right—Satyaki, King Virata, and the mighty King Drupada, renowned for his bravery...

...Dhrishtaketu, Chekitana, the valiant King of Kasi, Purujit, Kuntibhoja, and Saibya, the noblest of men...

...Yudhamanyu, strong and fierce, Uttamaujas, a warrior of great might, the son of Subhadra, Abhimanyu, and the sons of Draupadi, all courageous and heroic fighters.

Let me introduce you to the respected leaders of my army, who are esteemed among us. I want to make sure you know who they are, as they play important roles in our team.

Your Honour, we have warriors like Bhisma, Karna, and Krpa, who are known for their battlefield victories. There's also Ahsvatthama, Vikarna, Saumadatti, the son of Somadatta (Bhurishrava), and Jayadratha, among many others. All these skilled fighters, armed with a variety of weapons, are prepared to lay down their lives for me.

Our army, being larger and well-guarded by Bhisma, is unlikely to be overpowered. On the other hand, the army facing us, despite having Bhima as their protector, is more vulnerable and can be overwhelmed.

From your positions across the different divisions of the army, make sure to give special protection to Bhisma.

Bhisma, the revered grandfather of the Kuru family, known for his bravery, gave a mighty lion's roar and blew his conch to bring joy to Duryodhana.

Suddenly, conches, kettledrums, tabors, trumpets, and cow-horns erupted in a symphony of sound, shaking the very earth with their powerful blasts.

Krishna and Arjuna, seated together in their majestic chariot pulled by white horses, sounded their sacred conches.

Krishna blew the Panchajanya conch, while Arjuna sounded the Devadatta. Bhima, known for his fierce deeds and insatiable hunger, blew his massive conch, the Paundra.

King Yudhisthira, Kunti's son, blew his conch shell named Anantavijaya. Nakula and Sahadeva each sounded their conch shells as well, with Nakula's being Sughosha and Sahadeva's Manipushpaka.

King Dhritarashtra, ruler of the earth, listen! The king of Kashi, a master archer, the valiant Shikhandi, Dhrishtadyumna, and Virata, along with the unmatched Satyaki, King Drupada, the sons of Draupadi, and the powerful Abhimanyu, son of Subhadra—all of them blew their conches.

That awful sound echoed through the earth and sky, cutting straight to the hearts of Dhritarashtra's sons.

As the battle was about to commence, O ruler of the earth! Arjuna, with Hanuman on his banner, saw the sons of Dhritarashtra gathered on the battlefield. Raising his bow, he turned to Krishna and spoke these words.

Arjuna asked:

Achyuta, please position my chariot between the two armies. I want to see the warriors gathered here, eager for battle, and to get a clear look at those I will be fighting against at the start of this war.

I hope to see those who have come here to fight and who are determined to follow the wishes of Duryodhana, the one whose judgment is clouded.

Sanjaya said:

O King Bharata, as commanded by Gudakesha, Lord Krishna, who is also known as Hrshikesha, positioned the grand chariot right in the center of the battlefield, directly in front of Bhishma, Drona, and all the other rulers. He then addressed Arjuna, saying, 'Look at these Kauravas who have assembled here.'

Arjuna saw that among the two armies were his beloved paternal elders, grandfathers, teachers, uncles, brothers, sons, grandsons, friends, fathers-in-law, and even those who had always been his well-wishers.

Arjuna looked around at all the gathered relatives and, overwhelmed by deep compassion, spoke sorrowfully.

Arjuna said:

Krishna, as I look at these people—my own kin, ready and eager for battle—I'm overcome with weakness. My strength is leaving me, my mouth is dry, my body is shaking, and my hair stands on end.

My grip on Gandiva is slipping, and my skin feels like it's on fire. I can barely stand, and my mind is in utter disarray.

Keshava, I see many bad signs and can't find any good in fighting against our own people in this battle.

Krishna, I don't care about victory, a kingdom, or any comforts. Govinda! What good are these things to us—kingdoms, pleasures, or even life itself?

For the sake of those we desired the kingdom and all its pleasures, they have now come together for this battle, having given up their wealth and lives.

Here are the people we cherish: our teachers, paternal uncles, sons, grandfathers, maternal uncles, in-laws, grandsons, cousins, friends, and other beloved family members.

Madhusudana, I don't want to kill these people, even if it means they might kill me. Gaining control over the three worlds or even ruling this kingdom on earth isn't worth that to me.

Janardhana, what good could possibly come from defeating the sons of Dhritarashtra? All we would achieve is the accumulation of sin by vanquishing these wrongdoers.

How could we possibly find happiness in killing our own kin, the sons of Dhritarashtra? Destroying our own family, O Madhava, would only lead to our own sorrow.

O Janardhana, these people driven by greed can't see the harm they're causing by destroying families and betraying friends. But why don't we, who understand that such actions are the source of sin and suffering, step away from these wrongdoings?

When a family falls apart, its (dharma) traditional values and principles also disappear. And when these values are lost, won't wrongdoing take over and consume the entire family?

Krishna, as wrongdoing (adharma) increases, the women in our families will be led astray. When women lose their way, it brings chaos to society, O Varshneya!

Confusion can lead both the family and those who disrupt it into a world of suffering. Their ancestors, deprived of the proper rituals after death, face a fall from grace.

When people act in ways that harm families and create chaos in society, they undermine the timeless dharmas that families and communities rely on.

Janardhana, we've learned that in a world filled with suffering, those who disrupt the family's dharma are bound to face a life of hardship.

It's tragic that, driven by our desire for power and its luxuries, we're prepared to harm our own people and commit such a serious wrong.

It would be preferable for me if the sons of Dhritarashtra, armed and ready, were to defeat me—unarmed and non-resistant—on the battlefield.

Sanjaya said:

In the midst of the battlefield, Arjuna, overwhelmed with grief, set aside his bow and arrows and sat down on the chariot seat, consumed by sorrow.

CHAPTER TWO

Yoga of Understanding

Sankhya Yogah

Sanjaya described:

Seeing him so troubled and overwhelmed by compassion, his eyes brimming with tears and full of distress, Madhusudana spoke these comforting words.

Sri Bhagavan said:

Arjuna, where is this despair coming from in such a critical moment? It's not fitting for someone like you, and it won't bring you glory or lead you to a higher place.

Partha, don't give in to despair. This isn't like you, the great warrior who vanquishes enemies! Let go of this weakness and rise up with courage.

Arjuna said:

O Madhusudana, the destroyer of our enemies, how can I possibly fight against Bhishma and Drona with my arrows in this battle? They are so deserving of my respect and reverence.

It would be far more honorable to live off food given by others than to harm these cherished teachers. If I were to harm them, any enjoyment I find in this world would be tainted by their blood.

We're unsure whether it would be better for us to defeat them or for them to defeat us. The sons of Dhrtarashtra, whom we would rather not live to see defeated, are standing right in front of us.

Feeling overwhelmed and unsure about my path, I turn to you for guidance. Please help me understand what is truly best for me. As your student seeking refuge in your wisdom, I ask you to teach me.

Even if I were to gain an unparalleled kingdom on earth and rule over the heavens, I don't believe anything could ease the deep sorrow that leaves me feeling so empty.

Sanjaya described how Arjuna, the great warrior known for defeating enemies, spoke to Lord Krishna. He told Krishna, "I will not fight," and then fell silent.

O Bharata (Dhrtarashtra)! Amidst the two armies, when Arjuna was filled with sorrow, Lord Krishna, with a gentle smile, spoke these words to him.

Sri Bhagavan said:

You mourn for those who don't deserve your grief. Yet, you speak as if you have great wisdom. Truly wise people do not grieve for those who have departed or those who are yet to come.

There was never a time when I didn't exist, and the same goes for you and these kings. And none of us will ever truly cease to exist in the future.

Just as the jiva, or the indweller of the body, experiences stages like childhood, youth, and old age, it also transitions through different bodies over time. A wise person understands this and doesn't get distressed by it.

Arjuna, the sensations you experience through your senses—like warmth and cold, pleasure and pain—are fleeting and temporary. They come and go, so be patient and endure them.

Arjuna, you are a true leader among people! The one who remains unaffected by joy and sorrow, who stays steady in both pleasure and pain, and who has clear discernment, is truly prepared to attain liberation.

The unreal never truly exists, and the real never ceases to be. Those who understand the ultimate truth can see the difference between what is real and what is unreal.

Understand that the essence which permeates the entire world is truly indestructible. Nothing can destroy what remains constant and unchanging.

These bodies, belonging to the self that is unchanging and indestructible, and which cannot be known as an object, are said to come to an end. Therefore, Arjuna, rise and fight!

The one who believes the self can kill and the one who thinks it can be killed both misunderstand. The self neither kills nor is it killed.

The self is never born, nor does it die. It doesn't come into existence and then fade away. It is eternal, unchanging, and ever-present. Even when the body is destroyed, the self remains untouched.

Partha, the one who understands the self to be indestructible, timeless, unborn, and unchanging—how can that person kill anyone, or cause someone else to kill?

Just like we let go of old clothes and put on new ones, the self—the essence that lives within our bodies—lets go of old bodies and takes on new ones.

This self cannot be destroyed by weapons, nor can it be burned by fire. Water cannot drown it, and the wind cannot dry it.

This self cannot be destroyed by any means—it cannot be killed, burned, drowned, or dried up. It is unchanging, everywhere present, steady, unshakable, and eternal.

This true self is described as beyond appearance, beyond thought, and unchanging. So, understanding this, there's no reason to grieve.

And even if you think of the self (atman) as being subject to constant birth and death, Arjuna, mighty-armed warrior, you still shouldn't grieve for it in this way.

Everything that comes into existence is bound to face its end, and what has ended is sure to begin anew. So, it's best not to dwell on what you can't change.

Arjuna, all beings start in an unmanifest state, they take form in the middle of their journey, and then return to being unmanifest at the end. So, what is there really to be upset about?

Some people view the self as an incredible mystery. Others talk about it as if it were something truly astonishing. There are also those who hear about it and still find it completely unfathomable.

Arjuna, remember that the true self, or atman, within everyone is eternal and cannot be destroyed. So, there's no need for you to mourn for these people.

From your perspective, you must stay resolute. There's nothing more honorable for a warrior than fighting for the cause of righteousness.

Partha, only the fortunate kshatriyas have the chance to face a battle like this—one that comes by chance and opens the doors to heaven.

If you choose not to participate in this righteous battle, you're not only abandoning your own duty and honor but also risking the accumulation of sin.

People will talk endlessly about your lasting disgrace. For those who are honored, living with dishonor is often worse than death.

The great warriors will see your retreat from the battle as a sign of fear. Since they hold you in such high regard, this will cause them to lose respect for you.

Your enemies might say all sorts of hurtful things about you, trying to undermine your abilities. Is there anything more painful than that?

If you are defeated, you'll find peace in the afterlife; if you succeed, you'll enjoy the rewards of this world. So, Arjuna, rise up with determination and embrace the battle ahead.

Find contentment in both pleasure and pain, gain and loss, victory and defeat. Embrace these experiences with equanimity, and you will find yourself free from regret.

You've heard about Sankhya (self-knowledge) so far, Arjuna. Now, listen to the wisdom of yoga. Embracing this will help you free yourself from the constraints of your actions.

In this practice, no effort goes to waste, and it doesn't lead to negative outcomes. Even a small amount of this karma-yoga can shield you from immense fear.

Arjuna, descendant of the Kurus, when it comes to moksha (liberation), there's just one clear understanding. On the other hand, those who lack discernment have countless and varied opinions.

Partha, those who are deeply absorbed in the actions prescribed by the Vedas and their outcomes, who believe that nothing else exists beyond this, and who are driven by desires for heavenly rewards, speak in elaborate terms about various rituals. They emphasize these rituals as means to achieve pleasures, power, and better rebirths.

For those who chase after pleasure and power alone, and whose minds are captivated by these alluring distractions, true understanding never takes root.

The Vedas explore the concept of three fundamental qualities (gunas) that influence our lives. Arjuna, aim to rise above these qualities and the troubles they bring. Seek to remain calm and steady, unaffected by the swings of pleasure and pain. Strive to be grounded in clarity and wisdom (sattva), free from the worries of gaining and holding onto things, and become the master of your own mind and actions.

For a Brahmana who understands the true self, the Vedas are like a small reservoir in the midst of a flood—barely needed and almost redundant.

Your power lies in your actions, not in the outcomes. Don't believe you're in control of the results; instead, focus on what you can do, not what happens as a result. Avoid becoming attached to doing nothing.

Stay committed to yoga, Dhananjaya! Act without attachment, and maintain the same attitude towards success and failure. This balanced state of mind is what we call yoga.

Action driven solely by desire is less valuable compared to action performed with the right attitude of karma-yoga. Embrace this attitude of buddhi-yoga, Dhananjaya! Those who act only for the results are like misers.

Someone who remains steady and even-minded, regardless of their actions, transcends the effects of both good and bad deeds (papa and punya) in this life. So, embrace karma-yoga—which is the practice of wisdom and discretion in your actions.

Those who embrace the path of karma-yoga with wisdom, letting go of attachment to the results of their actions, and who are free from the cycle of rebirth, truly achieve a state that is free from all suffering.

When your mind moves beyond the confusion of delusion, you'll naturally develop a sense of detachment from both what you've heard and what you're yet to hear.

When your mind is no longer pulled in different directions by the Vedas, which offer various methods and goals, it will find stability and stay rooted in the self. This is when true self-knowledge will arise.

Arjuna asked:

Keshava, could you describe what someone with true wisdom (sthitaprajna) is like? How does a person who remains steady and undisturbed in themselves act—how do they speak, sit, and move through life?

Sri Bhagavan said:

When a person lets go of all desires as they arise in the mind and finds contentment solely within oneself, Partha, such a person is truly wise (sthitaprajna).

A wise person is someone who remains steady and unshaken even in the face of difficulties. They don't crave pleasure or let themselves be swayed by desire, fear, or anger. Their knowledge and wisdom are constant, unaffected by life's ups and downs.

Someone who remains unaffected by joy or sorrow, who doesn't get carried away by pleasant experiences or disturbed by unpleasant ones, has truly solidified their understanding.

A person who remains unaffected by all situations—neither celebrating when things go well nor resenting when they go poorly—has truly grounded knowledge.

When, just like a turtle retracts its limbs into its shell, this person can fully withdraw their senses from the external world, their understanding becomes steady and unwavering.

For someone who doesn't indulge their senses, the senses eventually turn inward, leaving behind a lingering desire. But once you've truly realized your own essence, or seen Brahman, even that desire fades away.

Even the person who is determined and clear-sighted can find their mind pulled away by the powerful forces of the senses, Kaunteya.

Let someone who has the ability to discern, and who has mastered control over their senses, sit in meditation on Me. For those who have achieved mastery over their senses, true understanding becomes firmly established.

When someone fixates on external things, they develop attachments to them. These attachments lead to desires, which in turn can spark anger. Anger clouds judgment, causing confusion and a loss of clarity. This loss of clarity erases memories and weakens the mind, ultimately leading to the person's downfall.

A person who has mastered their mind and navigates the world with their senses well-managed, free from strong likes and dislikes, finds true peace.

For someone with a calm mind, all pain and sorrow fade away. When the mind is at peace, knowledge becomes deep and enduring.

For someone who lacks tranquility, true understanding remains out of reach. Without tranquility, there can be no meaningful contemplation, and without contemplation, peace cannot be achieved. And if peace is absent, how can one find happiness?

When the mind chases after wandering senses, it takes away a person's wisdom, much like the wind drifts a small boat on the water.

Arjuna, strong and brave, when a person's senses are fully under control and not swayed by their surroundings, their knowledge remains steady and unwavering.

In the darkness that seems to surround everyone, the wise person who has mastered themselves remains awake and aware. Conversely, what others consider as daytime, filled with activity and awareness, feels like night to the wise individual who truly sees beyond appearances.

Just like water flowing into a vast and calm ocean, a wise person, who welcomes all experiences without being disturbed, finds inner peace. In contrast, someone who constantly craves more will never truly find tranquility.

A person who has let go of all their strong desires and moves through life without yearning or feeling a sense of ownership or limitation experiences true peace.

Arjuna, this is what it means to truly be immersed in Brahman. Once you have attained this state, you are free from delusion. By staying in this realization, even until the end of your life, you will achieve liberation.

CHAPTER THREE

Yoga of Action

Karma Yogah

Arjuna asked:

O Janardhana, if you believe that knowledge is superior to action, why then do you urge me to engage in this dreadful battle, O Keshava?

Your words seem to be pulling me in different directions, leaving me confused. Please, help me make up my mind and guide me toward the one thing that will lead to my liberation (shreyas).

Sri Bhagavan said:

O Anagha, from the very beginning, I have taught a two-fold committed lifestyle in this world—the lifestyle of jnana yoga for the contemplatives seeking direct realization, and the lifestyle of karma yoga for those who engage in action.

A person doesn't reach a state of true peace or inaction simply by avoiding actions. Likewise, true fulfillment or liberation isn't achieved just by renouncing the world and becoming a sannyasi.

No one can stay inactive, even for a moment, because everyone is driven to act by the three qualities of nature—sattva, rajas, and tamas—that arise from prakrti (nature).

A person who outwardly controls their actions but keeps dwelling on sensory pleasures in their mind is deceiving themselves and can be considered as someone with insincere behavior.

Arjuna, the person who controls their senses with their mind, stays detached, and practices the yoga of action through disciplined effort, is truly superior.

Take action because doing something is always better than doing nothing. Even maintaining your own health would be impossible without taking action.

If actions are not performed as a selfless offering to the Divine, a person remains entangled in the cycle of karma. Therefore, Arjuna, free yourself from attachment and act with the intention of offering your actions to the Divine (yajna).

At the start, the Creator, who brought humans into existence along with the practice of yajna, declared: 'Through this yajna you will grow and prosper. Let this yajna be like a wish-fulfilling cow for you.'

Offer your devotion to the deities through this ritual. May they, in turn, bless you. By honoring each other in this way, you will achieve the greatest good and liberation.

By performing yajna (sacrificial rites), we honor the deities and in return, they grant us the things we desire. If someone enjoys the blessings and gifts from the deities without giving anything back in gratitude, they are like a thief who takes without paying.

People who offer their food to the Lord before eating are cleansed of impurities. On the other hand, those who cook only for their own pleasure accumulate sin.

Life begins with food; food comes from rain; rain is the result of our good deeds; and those good deeds stem from our actions.

May you come to see that karma—whether it's ritual, prayer, or other practices—originates from the Veda, and the Veda itself comes from the imperishable (akshara). Therefore, the all-pervading Brahman is always present in the yajna (acts of sacrifice).

Partha, someone who doesn't align with the natural order of life and instead indulges only in sensory pleasures and sins is essentially wasting their life.

For someone who finds joy, satisfaction, and contentment within themselves, there is nothing more they need to seek or achieve.

For someone who finds deep joy in themselves, there's no real purpose in this world tied to doing or not doing things. They don't rely on anyone or anything for their sense of fulfillment.

So, always do what needs to be done to the best of your ability, but do it without clinging to the outcome. By focusing on your actions, without being attached to the results, you'll achieve the highest level of fulfillment.

Janaka and others achieved liberation through their actions alone. Similarly, recognizing the importance of guiding people away from harmful paths should inspire you to act.

People tend to follow the actions and decisions of those they consider important. Whatever an influential person deems right, others are likely to adopt as well.

Partha, for me, there's nothing left to achieve. In all the realms of existence, I've accomplished everything that can be achieved. Despite this, I continue to take action.

Arjuna, if I were to avoid taking action and be lazy, everyone would follow my example and do the same.

If I didn't take action, these people would suffer. I'd only create chaos and lead to their downfall.

Arjuna, just as those who lack wisdom act with a strong attachment to the outcomes, so too would the wise act—though without attachment. The wise are motivated by the desire to act for the benefit and protection of others.

A person who truly understands the self (the atman) should avoid disrupting the beliefs of those who are still focused on the outcomes of their actions. Instead, the wise individual, who is grounded in this knowledge and performs actions skillfully themselves, should gently guide and encourage others to act in the same way.

Actions are carried out by our body, mind, and senses in different ways, driven by the gunas of nature. However, when we're caught up in the ego, we mistakenly believe that 'I am the one doing everything'.

O Arjuna, powerful warrior! The one who understands the true nature of the gunas, is not bound by them. He knows that these gunas manifest in the body, mind, and senses, but he remains free from their influence.

People who get caught up in the changes of nature often become entangled with their physical and mental experiences and actions. Those who understand their true self should be careful not to disturb or criticize those who haven't yet reached that understanding and lack discernment.

Act with a clear and discerning mind, letting go of all attachment to the outcome. Don't worry about what the future holds or whether something is 'yours.' Approach your actions without anger or frustration, and simply do what needs to be done.

Those who faithfully follow my teachings, without criticizing the teachings or the teacher, will also be liberated from the consequences of their actions and attain freedom (moksha).

Those who criticize this teaching without good reason, who reject my vision, and who are confused in all areas of knowledge and lack discernment, can be seen as having lost their way.

Even a wise person will act according to their own nature. Since everyone follows their own nature, what's the point of trying to control them?

Every sense object carries both desire and aversion. Let us not fall under their influence, as they are our adversaries.

It's better to follow your own path (dharma), even if it's done imperfectly, than to excel in someone else's path. Facing the end while staying true to your own path is far preferable. Trying to live up to someone else's path is often filled with anxiety and fear.

Arjuna asked:

O Krishna, what makes a person commit sin, as if driven by some force, even when they don't want to?

Sri Bhagavan said:

This desire and anger, which come from the quality of rajas, are like a ravenous beast and a great sinner. Understand that they are the true enemies in this world.

Just as fire gets obscured by smoke, a mirror by dust, and a fetus by the womb, so too is knowledge obscured by the veil of desire.

Knowledge (jnanam) is often obscured by this unquenchable fire of desire, which is a perpetual challenge for the wise, Kaunteya!

Its presence is believed to reside in the senses, the mind, and the intellect. Through these, desire (kama) can cloud a person's judgment and obscure their wisdom.

O Bharatarshabha, you must first master your senses and then confront and overcome this wrongdoer, who is a threat to knowledge and wisdom.

It is said that our senses are more advanced than our physical body, and our mind surpasses our senses. The intellect, in turn, is higher than the mind. However, there is something even greater than the intellect, and that is the true self or atman.

Arjuna, with your great strength, understand this higher wisdom that goes beyond mere intellect. Steady your mind with this deeper insight and overcome the enemy of desire, which is so challenging to grasp and control.

O strong and valiant Arjuna! By understanding that which goes beyond mere intellect, and by calming your mind with wisdom, conquer the inner enemy, which takes the form of deep-seated desires that are hard to grasp and control.

CHAPTER FOUR

Renouncing Action through Wisdom

Jnana-Karma-Sannyasa-Yogah

Sri Bhagavan said:

I imparted this eternal yoga to Vivasvan, who then passed it on to Manu. Manu taught it to Ikshvaku. Through the generations, this wisdom was known to the wise kings. However, Arjuna, over time, this yoga has faded from the world.

Today, I've shared this timeless wisdom with you because you are both my devoted friend and follower. It truly is a deep and profound secret.

Arjuna said:

You were born only recently, while Vivasvan was born a long time ago. How can I be sure that you actually shared this knowledge with him in the distant past?

Sri Bhagavan said:

Arjuna, both you and I have lived through countless lifetimes. I remember them all, but you, brave warrior, do not.

Even though I am timeless and beyond birth, and I am the Lord of all life, I still create the illusion of coming into being through my own power (maya) and nature.

Arjuna, whenever you see that righteousness is fading and wrongdoing is on the rise, I come into the world in a physical form to restore balance and guide people back to the right path.

I appear in every age to safeguard those who uphold righteousness, to bring an end to those who embrace wrongdoing, and to establish a just and moral order (dharma).

The one who truly understands the divine nature of My birth and actions, Arjuna, upon leaving this body, is not reborn. Instead, they will reach Me.

Many have found their true nature by letting go of desire, fear, and anger. By placing their trust in me and purifying themselves through the practice of wisdom (jnana yoga), they have returned to who they truly are.

However people choose to worship me, I bless them in that very way. Arjuna, everyone walks my path in their own unique way.

People seek the outcomes of their actions in this world by worshipping various gods because, in the human realm, the results of their efforts manifest quickly.

The fourfold division of society was created by Me, based on the distinctions of qualities (gunas) and actions (karma). Though I am the creator of this system, know Me to be the non-doer and eternal.

I am not affected by actions or their outcomes. I don't have any desire or attachment to the results of what happens. Someone who understands me this way will not be trapped by their actions.

Understanding me this way, even the seekers of ancient times acted. So, follow their example and take action just as those who came before you did in the past.

Even the wise and learned are often puzzled about what truly constitutes action and what represents inaction. I'm here to explain the nature of action in a way that will free you from the misfortunes of worldly existence (samsara).

Understanding the actions prescribed by the scriptures is important. It's also crucial to be aware of actions that are forbidden and the concept of inaction. This is because the nature of karma can be quite complex and challenging to grasp.

The person who can see the stillness within action and recognize the activity within stillness is truly wise. This individual is a true yogin, having achieved all that needs to be done.

A person who acts without any attachment or desire, whose actions are guided by deep wisdom, is considered truly wise by the sages.

By letting go of a strong attachment to the outcomes of their actions, staying content with what they have, and not relying on anything external, a person can remain fully engaged in their work without feeling like they're actually doing anything.

A person who has let go of all expectations, who has mastered their body, mind, and senses, and who has given up all material possessions while focusing only on actions necessary to sustain their body, lives without sin.

The person who finds joy in whatever comes their way, remains steady regardless of life's ups and downs, and is free from jealousy, stays balanced in both success and failure—they are truly free, even while actively engaging in life.

The actions of someone who is free from attachment, liberated, grounded in self-knowledge, and performs daily duties as an offering to the divine (yajna), dissolve completely.

The process of offering is Brahman, the offering itself is Brahman, and it is Brahman who makes the offering into the fire that is also Brahman. When one perceives everything as Brahman, they attain Brahman.

Karma-yogins engage in rituals that call upon the deities, while sannyasins dedicate themselves entirely to the fire of Brahman through the pursuit of self-knowledge.

Some people sacrifice their sense of hearing and other senses into the fire of self-discipline, while others offer up sounds and other sensory experiences into the fire of their senses.

Others offer all their sensory experiences and actions into the fire of self-discipline, ignited by the light of knowledge.

Similarly, there are those who generously share their wealth, those who follow a disciplined path of prayer, those who practice yoga, and those who, with strong resolve and dedication, seek wisdom through the recitation of their sacred texts and the pursuit of self-knowledge.

Similarly, those dedicated to pranayama (breath control) focus on the balance between inhalation and exhalation. They harmonize the outgoing breath with the incoming breath, blending each into the other seamlessly.

People who control their food intake are essentially offering their craving for more food to the digestive fires within them. Those who follow religious practices, without exception, are those who have purified their minds through this ritualistic offering.

Arjuna, greatest of the Kurus! Those who enjoy the leftover nectar from the sacrifices reach the eternal Brahman. If someone doesn't participate in these sacrifices, they gain nothing in this world. So, how could they expect to gain anything in the next?

The Veda describes a wide range of religious practices in great detail. Recognize that these practices arise from karma (and are thus not the true self). By understanding this, you will attain liberation.

Arjuna, mighty conqueror of enemies! This pursuit of self-knowledge surpasses any religious rites involving material offerings. O Partha, all actions ultimately find their resolution in this wisdom.

To truly understand, approach those who are wise with humility. Ask thoughtful questions and offer your service. These enlightened individuals, who see the truth clearly, will guide you in gaining this Jnanam (self-knowledge).

Arjuna, with this jnana that they have imparted to you, you will no longer be confused or misled. By understanding this wisdom, you'll be able to see all beings both within yourself and within Me.

No matter how far you've strayed, even if you feel like the greatest sinner, you'll overcome all your transgressions effortlessly with the guidance of knowledge.

Arjuna, just like a bright fire turns wood into ashes, the fire of jnana burns away the results of all actions.

In this world, there's nothing that purifies the mind quite like self-knowledge. One who is perfected in yoga realizes this truth in time within oneself.

A person who has faith in the teachings of the scriptures and the guidance of their teacher, who is dedicated to this knowledge, and who has mastery over their senses, will attain true understanding. With this understanding comes a profound and immediate sense of inner peace.

Someone who lacks discernment, has no faith in the teachings or the teacher, and is plagued by doubt will ultimately face ruin. For someone with a doubting mind, neither this world nor the next holds any meaning, and happiness remains out of reach.

Dhananjaya, actions no longer bind someone who has embraced the path of yoga, whose uncertainties have been completely resolved through wisdom, and who remains steadfast and centered.

Bharata, you must overcome this doubt about your true self, which comes from ignorance and is deeply rooted in your mind, with the sword of knowledge. Rise up and embrace the path of yoga.

CHAPTER FIVE

Renunciation

Sannyasa Yogah

Arjuna said:

Krishna, you speak highly of both renouncing actions and yoga of action. Please, tell me clearly which of these paths is the better one.

Sri Bhagavan said:

Both renouncing action (sannyasa) and performing action as a form of yoga can lead to liberation. However, among these two paths, practicing action as yoga is considered superior to simply renouncing action.

Arjuna, mighty warrior, consider someone who neither hates nor desires anything as truly a renunciate (sannyasi). Such a person, free from the swings of like and dislike, is naturally free from the constraints of attachment.

While those who lack understanding might argue that sankhya and yoga are separate paths, the truth is that someone who genuinely practices even one of these paths will experience the benefits of both.

The ultimate goal (moksha) achieved by sannyasins can also be reached by yogins. The person who understands that sankhya and yoga are essentially the same truly perceives the truth.

Arjuna, giving up action is a tough path without practicing yoga. But someone who dedicates themselves to yoga and has a sharp mind will quickly achieve a deep understanding of the Brahman.

A person who dedicates themselves to a life of selfless action, whose mind is clear and disciplined, who has control over their body and senses, and who sees themselves as the same self present in everyone, remains unaffected by their actions.

The person who is truly aware understands that, even though they see, hear, touch, smell, eat, walk, sleep, breathe, ...

...talk, release, grasp, open, and close their eyes, they realize that they themselves are not actively doing any of these things. Instead, they see that their senses and actions are simply engaging with the world around them.

One who performs actions, offering them to Brahman and renouncing attachment, is not tainted by sin, just as a lotus leaf is untouched by water.

Yogins let go of attachment and perform their actions purely, without being driven by personal preferences or aversions. They engage their body, mind, intellect, and senses in their work to purify their minds.

Someone who practices yoga by letting go of the results of their actions will find a sense of calm and balance, rooted in their dedication to this way of living. On the other hand, someone who is driven by desires and lacks this commitment will find themselves entangled, clinging to the outcomes of their efforts.

The self within the body, who is master of their own mind and has mentally renounced all actions through wisdom, finds contentment living within the body's nine gates. This person neither engages in actions themselves nor compels others to act.

The Atman doesn't create actions or doership, nor does it connect with the outcomes of actions. Instead, it's one's own nature that guides and leads to action.

The Atman isn't affected by anyone's good or bad deeds. It remains untouched by their karma. However, ignorance can obscure this understanding, causing people to be misled and confused about their true nature.

For those who have gained self-knowledge, it's as if the darkness of ignorance has been lifted. Just like the sun reveals everything hidden in darkness, this Jnanam (self-knowledge) unveils the true self, which is Brahman.

Those who truly understand the essence of Brahman, who see their true self as this divine reality, and who are fully dedicated to this understanding, achieve a state of enlightenment. For them, the ultimate goal has already been reached, and their ignorance has been cleared away by Jnanam. They reach a profound state of liberation from which there is no return.

Wise are those who recognize the same divine essence in everyone, whether it's in a learned and humble Brahmin, in a cow, an elephant, a dog, and even in someone who eats dogs.

In this life, those who find their minds rooted in the essence that unites all things—what we call Brahman—overcome the cycle of birth and death. Because Brahman is flawless and constant, those who understand this live in harmony with it.

The person who truly understands Brahman and is firmly grounded in this knowledge, free from delusions, remains steady and untroubled. They neither delight in acquiring what is desirable nor become upset by what is undesirable.

Someone who isn't overly attached to external things finds a certain happiness within themselves. However, if their mind is filled with the understanding of Brahman, they experience a happiness that never fades.

Arjuna, the wise know that pleasures from physical sensations and objects are fleeting and often lead to pain. Since they have a start and an end, a wise person doesn't get lost in them.

One who is able to endure here in this life the urges of desires and anger arising from the body, is considered a person who is truly united in yoga and thus is happy.

A person who finds complete fulfillment within themselves, who delights in their own being, and who is fully aware of their true self, is the one who truly understands that their essence is Brahman. Such a wise individual attains the freedom that is Brahman.

Sages who have cleared their inner impurities, resolved their doubts, achieved self-mastery, and are joyfully dedicated to the well-being of all beings, attain liberation.

For those sannyasins who have conquered desire and anger, who have mastered their own minds, and who truly understand their inner self, there is freedom and liberation in this life as well as beyond.

By focusing inward and keeping eyes gently closed, with breath flowing evenly through nostrils, a person who has mastered their actions, senses, mind, and intellect, and who sees liberation as their ultimate goal—free from desire, fear, and anger—truly experiences freedom and liberation.

By recognizing Me as the one who upholds rituals and disciplines, the master of all realms, and a friend to every being, one attains peace and liberation.

CHAPTER SIX

Meditation

Dhyana Yogah

Sri Bhagavan said:

The true sannyasi (renunciant) and yogi is the one who performs their duties without attachment to the results, not just someone who has given up rituals and external actions.

What is often called renunciation, Arjuna, is actually the practice of karma yoga. Understand that one who hasn't let go of desires for limited outcomes, like heaven and similar rewards, cannot truly be a karma yogi.

For someone striving to achieve a meditative state through yoga, practicing karma yoga is the path. However, for someone who has already reached that state of yoga, complete renunciation is seen as the way forward.

When someone is free from attachment to both worldly pleasures and their actions, they are considered to have attained liberation, having let go of the root of all desires.

Raise yourself up with your own efforts, and don't bring yourself down. Your own self is your best friend, but it can also be your worst enemy.

When one has mastered oneself, the self becomes their own best friend. But when one fails to gain self-mastery, the self turns into an enemy, acting just like one.

For someone who has mastered self-control and remains calm in the face of heat or cold, pleasure or pain, praise or criticism, their mind stays balanced and composed no matter the circumstances.

A person who finds inner peace through self-knowledge (jnana-vijnana-triptatma), remains steady and unshaken, and has control over their senses and actions—someone who sees a lump of earth, a stone, and gold with equal detachment—is called a yogin.

The person who sees everyone—whether they are a benefactor, a friend, an enemy, an acquaintance, an arbitrator, someone they dislike, a relative, a kind soul, or even a sinner—with the same level of compassion and respect, is truly remarkable and exalted.

Let the meditator, with a calm body and mind, free from desires and possessions, find a peaceful place to be alone. There, let them consistently focus their mind on the object of their meditation.

After setting up your seat with a soft cloth, a layer of skin, and a grass mat in that order, make sure the place is clean, firm, and at a comfortable height—not too high or too low....

.... Sit down on this seat and focus your mind completely on the object of meditation. The one who has mastered their mind and senses should then practice meditation to purify the mind.

Remain steady and unmoving, with your body, head, and neck aligned as if you're gazing at the tip of your nose, keeping your eyes focused and avoiding looking around. Be someone whose mind is calm and fearless, dedicated to the path of a brahmacharin. Let that meditator sit, with Me as their ultimate goal, withdrawing their mind from all distractions and focusing solely on Me.

When the meditator consistently focuses the mind this way, they achieve a profound peace that is centered on Me. This peace, which involves being absorbed in Me, represents the ultimate liberation (parama-nirvana).

Meditation isn't suited for someone who overeats or who never eats at all, Arjuna. It's also not for someone who sleeps excessively or who is constantly awake. Instead, it's for those who find a balanced approach to both food and rest.

For someone who maintains balance in their eating, activities, and overall lifestyle—being aware and mindful in both waking and sleeping hours—meditation becomes a powerful tool for overcoming sorrow.

When the mind finds a deep sense of calm and stays focused on the true self, and when one is no longer driven by cravings or desires, that person is considered to have truly achieved mastery.

A lamp shielded from the wind remains steady and calm. Similarly, this example is used to describe the serene and stable mind of a meditator who is engaged in self-reflection and contemplation.

When the mind is tamed through meditation and finds peace within itself, and when you see and appreciate your true self for what it is, you find joy in being who you truly are...

...when you come to understand this deep and lasting happiness that the mind can grasp, beyond what our senses can tell us, and when you stay grounded in this truth, never straying from your true self...

When you achieve this state, you'll realize there's nothing greater to attain. Once you're established in this state, you won't be shaken even by the deepest sorrows.

Understanding this detachment from sorrow is what yoga truly means. Pursue this yoga with a clear purpose and a steadfast mind, never letting discouragement hold you back.

Let go of all desires that come from your thoughts, and withdraw your senses and actions through sheer mental focus. With determination, allow your intellect to gradually calm your mind. Focus your mind entirely on the self and avoid thinking about anything else.

Even though the mind is constantly shifting and unsettled, you can bring it back under control. By focusing on the self and by your own inner strength, you can guide your mind to be more steady and centered.

The greatest joy comes to a meditator whose mind is calm, whose inner impurities have been cleared, whose life is free from flaws, and who has attained unity with Brahman through wisdom.

A person who meditates, free from the struggles that come from living unethically, naturally connects their mind with their object of meditation. In doing so, they effortlessly experience the profound joy that comes from recognizing their unity with Brahman.

A person who reflects deeply and achieves clarity of mind will see that everything is interconnected. They perceive themselves in all beings and recognize all beings within themselves.

To the person who sees Me in everyone and sees everyone in Me, I am always close, and they are always close to Me.

Someone who perceives the unity of me within all beings and recognizes this oneness—such a yogin remains connected to me, no matter what they do.

Arjuna, the yogin who sees pleasure and pain as equal by using their own experience as a reference, is considered the highest among yogis.

Arjuna said:

Krishna, you've spoken about this yoga of equanimity, but I'm struggling to grasp its steady vision because my mind is restless and agitated.

Indeed, Krishna, the mind is like a powerful and deeply entrenched tyrant. I find it as hard to control as the wind.

Sri Bhagavan said:

Arjuna, you're right—the mind can be restless and hard to control. But remember, Kaunteya, with persistent practice and maintaining objectivity, you can gain mastery over it.

Yoga can be challenging for someone who hasn't yet learned to control their mind. This is my perspective. However, it becomes attainable for those who have mastered their mind and put in the effort with the right approach - through consistent practice and objectivity.

Arjuna asked:

Krishna, what happens to someone who believes in the teachings of the scriptures but doesn't put in enough effort, and whose mind drifts away from their practice of yoga? If they don't succeed in their efforts, where do they end up?

O Krishna, mighty-armed, what becomes of one who is confused on the path to knowing Brahman? Lost between two worlds, with no firm ground to stand on, does such a person, like a cloud scattered and broken, fade away without direction or purpose?

Krishna, please clear this doubt of mine completely. There's no one else but you who can dispel it.

Sri Bhagavan said:

Partha, there is no ruin for anyone who walks the path of righteousness, neither in this life nor the next. Those who perform good deeds will never meet a bad end.

After enjoying the rewards of good deeds for many years in higher realms, those who didn't fully achieve success in yoga are reborn into a family of wealth and virtue, where dharma is deeply valued.

Or he is born into the family of wise yogis, a birth that is truly rare and difficult to attain in this world.

There, he connects with the wisdom from his previous life and works towards achieving even greater success in yoga than before, Arjuna, the pride of the Kuru family!

Through this earlier practice alone, he is naturally drawn to yoga. Just as someone seeking the knowledge of yoga will eventually move beyond the ritualistic aspects of the Vedas.

A yogin who diligently works with determination can purify themselves of all the impurities accumulated from countless past lives. Through this effort, they ultimately achieve their highest goal.

A yogi is regarded as more advanced than those who solely practice meditation, even more enlightened than scholars, and beyond those who just take action. So, Arjuna, strive to be a yogi.

Among all those who practice yoga, the one who has deep faith and a mind fully focused on Me, who contemplates on Me with devotion, is the highest of them all. This is how I see it.

CHAPTER SEVEN

Indirect and Immediate Knowledge

Jnana-Vijnana Yogah

Sri Bhagavan said:

Arjuna, with your mind devoted to Me through the practice of yoga and having fully surrendered to Me, listen carefully as I reveal how you can come to know Me completely and without any doubt.

I will teach you everything without holding anything back—both knowledge (jnanam) and the immediate insight (vijnanam) that comes with it. Once you understand this, there will be nothing else left for you to learn in this world.

Out of thousands of people, only a rare individual strives for liberation. And even among those dedicated seekers, only a few truly come to know Me as I am.

The Earth, water, fire, air, space, mind, intellect, and the sense of self—all these elements make up my prakriti (nature), divided into eight parts.

Arjuna, mighty warrior, this is my lower nature. But beyond this, please understand my higher nature, which is the true essence of the self—the force that sustains this entire world.

Recognize that everything in existence—every being and every element—originates from this dual nature of the universe. I am the source from which the entire world emerges, and I am also the ultimate destination into which everything returns.

Dhananjaya, there's nothing greater than Me. Everything you see is like beads strung together, all woven into me.

Kaunteya, I am the flavor you experience in water, the light that shines in the moon and the sun, I am the sacred sound 'Om' in the Vedas, the sound that resonates in the vastness of space, and the strength that resides within every person.

I am the gentle scent that rises from the earth, the warmth and glow in the fire. I am the life force that breathes through all beings and I am the spiritual practices and their fruits experienced by the ascetics.

Partha, recognize that I am the eternal essence within all beings. I am the wisdom in those who can discern, and I am the inner light that shines through the brilliant.

Arjuna, you're the greatest among the Bharatas! In those who are strong, I am the inner strength that remains free from longing and attachment. Among all beings, I am the pure desire that aligns with righteousness (dharma).

Everything that comes from the qualities (gunas) of sattva, rajas, and tamas is ultimately created by Me. While they exist within Me, I am not confined by them.

This whole world is caught up in the changing nature of the three gunas and doesn't recognize Me as the eternal and unchanging reality beyond these changes.

This maya(illusion), which comes from Me and is shaped by the three gunas of nature, is hard to overcome.

But those who seek Me with sincerity will be able to transcend this maya.

People who act wrongly and are misled, those who are lost in their ways, often don't seek me. They're caught up in the maya and are distracted by their own desires, living a life focused solely on sensory pleasures.

Bharatarshabha! People who come to me with good intentions fall into four categories: those who are troubled and seeking relief, those who are looking for safety and happiness, those who want to understand me, and those who already know me (jnani).

Among them, the jnani, the person who truly knows and is always connected to Me and whose devotion is focused on our unity, stands out because I hold him dear, and he holds Me dear in return.

All of these individuals are certainly admirable, but it's the jnani who truly understands and sees things as I do. This is my perspective. The person whose mind is fully absorbed in me has truly reached me—the ultimate destination where there is no further end.

After many lifetimes, someone who truly understands that 'Vasudeva is everything' eventually finds their way to Me. Such a wise person is incredibly rare.

People whose judgment is clouded by their own desires and inclinations end up worshiping different gods according to what they've been taught.

No matter who the devotee is or which form they choose to worship with genuine faith, I strengthen and support that faith for them.

Anyone who sincerely worships that deity with faith will receive the blessings and desires that I alone have planned for them.

For those who see things more clearly, the outcome is straightforward. Those who worship the deities go to the deities, while those who worship Me will come to Me.

People who lack discernment and don't understand my boundless and unchanging nature may see me, though I am formless, as having a distinct form.

Under the influence of yoga-maya, I remain hidden from many. Those who are misled don't understand Me as the eternal and unchanging one.

Arjuna, I understand every being that has ever lived, exists now, or will come into existence. Yet, despite this, no one truly knows Me.

Bharata, you who vanquish your foes! Everyone gets caught in confusion and delusion because of their desires and aversions, losing their way in this world.

People who lead good lives and have overcome their past wrongdoings, who have moved beyond the illusions of opposites and are steadfast in their devotion, ultimately find their way to Me.

Those who seek refuge in Me and strive for freedom from old age and death come to understand Brahman as their true self and gain a complete understanding of karma.

People who see Me in the physical world, the deities, and the rituals, and who keep their thoughts focused on Me, even as they reach the end of their lives, truly understand Me.

CHAPTER EIGHT

The Imperishable Brahman

Akshara-Brahma Yogah

Arjuna asked:

O Purushottama, what is Brahman? What is the nature of the self? What is karma? What is meant by being centered on all beings? And what does it mean to be centered on the gods?

Madhusudana, can you explain what it is within this body that is connected to rituals? And when someone is facing death with a calm and steady mind, how do they come to know you?

Sri Bhagavan said:

Brahman is the infinite, unchanging reality. When this limitless essence is expressed through the body, it is known as the jiva, or individual soul. Karma, which leads to the creation of new bodies for living beings, can be understood as an offering that perpetuates the cycle of birth and rebirth.

Arjuna, noble among all beings! Whatever is centered on living beings is bound to decay. What is centered on the gods is the cosmic essence, Hiranyagarbha. But within this body, I am the essence that upholds all rituals.

When someone leaves their body at the moment of death, holding Me in their thoughts, they attain My essence. There's no doubt about this.

Kaunteya, at the moment of death, a person will move towards whatever they've been thinking about or attached to throughout their life. If they have been focused on something in life, that's what they'll encounter in their final moments.

Keep me in your thoughts at all times and fight. When you dedicate your mind and heart to me, you will surely find your way to me. There's no doubt about it.

Partha, when you reflect deeply, keeping your mind focused on the teachings and practicing yoga without distraction, you will connect with the boundless, self-radiant essence of who you truly are.

The person who closes off all the senses, draws their mind inward to the heart, focuses their breath at the top of their head, and holds it there through yoga, while chanting the sacred sound Om, which represents Brahman, lets go of their physical body and leaves this world remembering Me reaches the highest state of existence.

Partha, the one who focuses solely on Me and constantly keeps Me in their thoughts, finds that I am easily accessible to them. For a yogi who remains always connected with Me, I am close at hand.

When wise people reach me, they no longer experience rebirth into the world of suffering and limitation. They have achieved the highest success.

Arjuna, every world, from the highest realm of Brahma to the lowest, is subject to change and rebirth. But when you reach Me, Kaunteya, you will be free from the cycle of rebirth.

People who understand the concept of day and night in the cosmic sense know that a day for Brahma consists of one thousand yugas, and his night is also one thousand yugas long.

At the start of each day, everything that exists emerges from the formless source. And as night falls, everything returns to that same formless origin.

Partha, the same beings that come into existence over and over again will naturally dissolve when Brahma's night falls. When the day arrives, they come into being once more.

However, there's a different kind of unmanifest that stands apart from the usual. This one is always present and eternal. Unlike everything else that can be destroyed, this eternal essence remains unaffected even when all other beings come to an end.

Arjuna, the limitless essence (purusha) that you seek can only be reached through devotion, where there is no other. This essence is the source of all beings and the presence that permeates everything around us.

Bharatarshabha, let me share with you the paths of no return and return—the routes that the yogis follow after they leave this world.

Leaving by the path where the deity of fire, the deity of light, the deity of the day, the deity of the bright fortnight of the moon, and the deity of the six months of the northern solstice reside, those who meditate on Brahman journey to the realm of Brahma.

The yogin, traveling along the path where the deities of clouds, night, the waning moon, and the six months of the southern solstice reside, reaches the moon's realm and then returns.

In the ancient scriptures, it's said that there are two eternal paths in life: the bright and the dark. One path leads to a place from which there's no return, while the other leads to a cycle of returning.

Arjuna, now that you understand these two paths, a true yogi is never deceived. So, always stay connected to yoga, Arjuna.

The yogin, understanding these answers, transcends all teachings found in sacred texts that focus on the outcomes of good deeds, such as Vedic study, rituals, disciplines, and acts of charity. And reaches the ultimate cause of creation, the highest state of existence.

CHAPTER NINE

The King of Knowledge, The King of Secrets

Rajavidya-Rajaguhya Yogah

Sri Bhagavan said:

Now, I will explain to you, without any distortion, this profound and most secret knowledge (jnana), along with the immediate understanding (vijnana) that comes with it. By knowing this, you will be freed from all that is inauspicious.

This is the most exalted knowledge, the most profound secret, and the supreme purifier. It is directly experienced, aligned with righteousness, easy to achieve, and everlasting.

Arjuna, mighty warrior! Those who lack faith in this self-knowledge cannot attain Me. Instead, they remain trapped in the endless cycle of life and death, bound by the road of samsara.

This entire world is infused with My presence, though My true form cannot be seen or grasped. All beings exist within Me, yet I am not confined to them.

And the beings don't actually reside in Me. See this divine mystery of how I am connected to the world. Though My true Self creates and sustains all beings, it does not dwell within them.

Just as the boundless air moves everywhere but always remains within the sky, in the same way, know that all beings exist within Me.

All beings, Arjuna, return to My nature when the cycle of creation comes to an end. And when the cycle begins again, I bring them forth once more.

By keeping My prakriti under control, I continually create all these beings, driven by the power of prakriti itself.

Dhananjaya, these actions don't tie me down. I'm like someone who is just watching from the sidelines, detached and unaffected by what happens.

With me overseeing everything, nature brings forth all that moves and all that stands still in the world. That's why, Kaunteya, you see the world constantly changing.

Those who are confused don't see Me as I truly am—present within every human body, unaware of My boundless nature as the Lord of all beings (Maheshwara).

People who are driven by unrealistic dreams, pointless actions, and shallow knowledge, and who lack discernment, end up adopting the deceitful ways of the rakshasas and asuras.

Partha, those with noble hearts, who have a deep spiritual nature and recognize Me as the eternal source of all life and elements, are wholeheartedly devoted to Me and seek Me out.

People who constantly appreciate Me, make the effort, stay committed, and remain devoted to Me with a sincere heart are the ones who truly seek Me.

Some people also honor Me through the ritual of knowledge. They see Me in many different ways: as a single, unified presence, and yet also as something diverse and distinct.

I am the ritual and the worship itself. I am the food that's offered and food in general. I am the chants and the essence of the ghee. I am the fire that fuels the ritual and the offering itself.

I am the parent of this world, both its father and mother. I provide for its needs and I am the source of all that exists. I am the ultimate truth to be understood, the one who cleanses and purifies. I am the the sacred sound of Om, and I am the essence of the Vedic scriptures—Rk, Sama, and Yajur Vedas.

I am the result of all actions and the source of nourishment. I am the ultimate guide and witness, providing a sanctuary and being inherently helpful. Everything in creation begins with me, returns to me, and exists within me. I am the foundation of everything, the eternal cause behind all that is.

I warm the world and control the rain, holding it back or letting it fall. I am both eternal and fleeting, embodying life and death. I am the force behind cause and effect, Arjuna!

Those who are well-versed in the three Vedas and perform the soma ritual to cleanse themselves of their sins, having honored Me through their ceremonies, seek to reach heaven. By accumulating merit through their righteous actions, they attain Indra's realm and experience the heavenly delights enjoyed by the celestial beings.

When people who have experienced the bliss of heaven run out of their good karma, they return to the earthly realm. In this way, those who pursue various goals by adhering to the rituals of the three Vedas find themselves caught in the cycle of repeated birth and rebirth, known as samsara.

People who see themselves as one with Me, and truly recognize Me, will come to know Me. For those who are always united with Me, I look after their needs and protect what they cherish.

Kaunteya, even those who sincerely worship other deities are actually honoring Me, though they may not realize it due to their ignorance.

I am the one who receives all the rituals and the only true Lord. Yet, they don't truly understand me, so they drift away.

People who dedicate themselves to the gods find their way to the realm of gods. Those who honor their ancestors journey to the world of the ancestors. Those who revere the spirits enter the realm of the spirits. But those who worship Me will come to Me.

Whoever offers me a leaf, a flower, a fruit, or water with genuine devotion, I accept that gift, recognizing the purity and sincerity of the person's heart.

No matter what you do, whether it's what you eat, the rituals you practice, the gifts you give, or the religious duties you follow, Kaunteya, make it all a way of offering it to me.

By following this path, you'll free yourself from the ties of karma, which brings both pleasant and unpleasant outcomes. With a mind steeped in detachment and yoga (sannyasa-yoga-yukta-atma), you'll achieve liberation and come to me.

I am the same in everyone, and I don't favor anyone over another. I have no dislikes or favorites. However, those who approach Me with genuine devotion find that I am present in them, just as they are in Me.

Even if someone with questionable behavior seeks me out without any sense of separation, they should still be seen as a good person. This is because their intention reveals a clear understanding, even if their actions don't always reflect it.

He swiftly becomes someone whose mind aligns with dharma and attains everlasting peace. Know this for sure, Kaunteya: my devoted follower will never be lost.

Certainly, Arjuna! Even those born into families with improper conduct, as well as women (not just men), Vaishyas, and Shudras, can achieve the ultimate goal by taking refuge in Me.

So, imagine the good fortune of the brahmanas who are born into fortunate circumstances and are devoted, as well as the wise kings (kshatriyas). Despite having attained this transient and only mildly happy world, may you still seek Me.

May you become someone whose heart and mind are fully devoted to Me. May you dedicate your actions and rituals to Me, and may you offer yourself in complete surrender. By preparing yourself in this way, with Me as your ultimate goal, you will find your way to Me, the true self.

CHAPTER TEN

Glories of the Lord

Vibhuti Yogah

Sri Bhagavan said:

Listen closely, Arjuna, mighty warrior, as I speak again for your benefit. I will reveal to you the boundless truth, as you take joy in My words.

Neither the gods nor the sages can fully comprehend the glory of My manifestation in this world because I am the source from which all gods and sages arise.

Whoever understands Me as the eternal, beginningless, and boundless Lord of the universe—beyond cause and effect—becomes free from delusion and is released from all sins.

All aspects of living beings, like the ability to understand, gain knowledge, and see clearly without confusion; the capacity to be open-minded, truthful, and self-controlled; the power to master one's thoughts; experiences of pleasure and pain; the forces of creation and destruction; feelings of fear and fearlessness; and further...

...qualities such as non-harming, calmness, contentment, spiritual discipline, generosity, fame, and even infamy—these various traits and experiences all originate from Me alone.

The seven ancient sages and the four Manus, whose minds are fully aligned with Me, are born from My mind. All living beings in the world have come from them.

Anyone who truly understands the depth of My greatness and My connection to it will have an unwavering vision. There's no question about that.

I am the source of everything, and it's because of me that everything continues to exist. By understanding this, wise individuals with insight come to know and connect with me.

Those who keep their thoughts on Me, find their purpose in Me, and share their experiences and conversations about Me with each other, are always content and find joy in everything they do.

For those who are always devoted to Me and seek Me with love, I grant them the vision to find Me.

Out of compassion for these sincere seekers, I illuminate their minds with the light of knowledge, dispelling the darkness of ignorance and freeing them from delusion.

Arjuna said:

O revered one, you are the boundless essence, the light beyond all lights, and the source of purity. The great sages—Narada, Asita, Devala, Vyasa, and others—speak of you as the eternal, transcendent being, the origin of all gods, who is both unborn and all-encompassing. And truly, you have confirmed this yourself.

Keshava, everything you've shared with me, I believe to be true. Even the gods and demons don't fully understand your true nature, Lord!

Only you, Purushottama, truly understand yourself with your own mind. You are the creator of all beings, the ruler of everyone, the supreme Lord of the Gods, and the master of creation!

You truly have the power to fully share the incredible greatness within you, the very greatness that fills and influences these worlds.

O greatest of yogis! I'm always wondering, how can I truly understand you? In what forms should I meditate on you, my Lord?

Could you once more share with me in detail the splendor and magnificence of yourself, Janardhana? I, who am savoring this divine nectar, find myself still yearning for more.

Sri Bhagavan answered:

Arjuna, you're the finest of the Kurus! Let me share with you the most important aspects of my divine nature. There's so much to say about my glories that I could never cover it all in detail.

Hey Gudakesha! I am the inner self present in everyone's heart, and I am the source behind the creation, maintenance, and ultimate resolution of everything.

Of the Adityas, I am Vishnu; among the shining stars, I am the Sun, with its radiant beams. Among the Maruts, I am Marichi, and when it comes to the night-time luminaries, I am the Moon.

Of all the Vedas, I am the Samaveda; among the gods, I am Indra. In terms of ways to understand and know, I am the mind itself, and among living beings, I am the power of awareness.

Of all the Rudras, I am Shankara; among the Yakshas and Rakshasas, I am Kubera; among the Vasus, I am Fire; and among the snow-capped mountains, I am Meru.

Partha, recognize Me as Brhaspati, the foremost among the priests. Among the great leaders, I am Skanda, and when it comes to bodies of water, I am the ocean.

Among the wise, I am Bhrgu; among words, I am the sacred syllable Om; among rituals, I am the practice of japa, and among mountains, I am the majestic Himalayas.

I am like the sacred fig tree among all trees; among the celestial sages, I am Narada; among the celestial musicians, I am Chitraratha; and among the enlightened beings, I am the sage Kapila.

Among horses, think of me as Ucchaihshravas, and among elephants, as Airavata—both of which emerged from the churning of the ocean for nectar. And among people, I am the king.

Of all the weapons, I am the mighty Vajra. Among cows, I am the wish-fulfilling Kamadhenu. I am Kandarpa, the deity of love who inspires creation. And among the poisonous serpents, I am the great Vasuki.

I am Ananta, the great serpent among the many-headed snakes. I am Varuna, the chief among the gods of water. I am Aryama, the noble one among the ancestors, and I am Yama, the enforcer of discipline.

I am Prahlada among the daityas, the demons born from Diti. I embody Time among all things that measure, the lion among wild animals, and Garuda among the birds.

Of all things that purify, I am like the fresh, cleansing air. I am like Rama among warriors, the most powerful among them. In the world of fish, I am the formidable shark, and among rivers, I am the sacred Ganges.

Arjuna, I am the source, the essence, and the ultimate goal of all creation. In the realm of knowledge, I represent the understanding of the self. And among those who engage in discussion, I am the conversation that guides you toward the truth.

In the alphabet, I am the letter 'a,' and in the realm of compound words, I represent the dvandva (dual compound). I am time itself, endless and existing forever and always. I am the one who provides the results of actions and is present everywhere.

I am Death, the force that ultimately takes everything away, but I also bring new beginnings and prosperity to those who come after. In the realm of feminine qualities, I embody fame, wealth, eloquence, memory, intelligence, strength, and balance.

I am the Brhatsama among all the hymns, the Gayatri among the verses, Margashirsa among the months, and Spring among the seasons.

I am the game of dice among things that deceive; I represent the brilliance among the brightest. I embody the victory of those who triumph. I am the clarity in thinking for those who possess it. Among those with a nature predominantly shaped by goodness, I am their pure, contemplative quality (sattva guna).

Among the Yadavas, I am Vasudeva; among the Pandavas, I am Arjuna; among the sages, I am Vyasa; and among the wise teachers, I am the revered Ushana.

I am the authority that enforces order; I am the strategy of those who seek to win. I am silence among the secrets. I am knowledge of the enlightened.

Arjuna, I am the source of everything that exists. Nothing, whether it's moving or still, living or non-living, can exist without me.

Arjuna, there is no limit to My amazing glories! But I've only shared a few of the most significant ones with you.

Everything that exists with splendor, wealth, or power is just a glimpse of My glory.

But, Arjuna, what does this partial understanding really achieve for you? Know this fully: I am present everywhere in the world through just a small part of My being.

CHAPTER ELEVEN

Vision of the Cosmic Form

Vishvarupa Darshana Yogah

Arjuna said:

By your grace, Lord, and through the wisdom you've shared about the greatest secret—the knowledge of the self—my confusion has been dispelled.

I have heard in detail from you, Krishna, about how things and beings are created and dissolved. Your words, spoken by you with eyes as beautiful as lotus petals, have also revealed your timeless glory.

Just as you've spoken about yourself, Lord, I now yearn to see your divine form, O Purushottama!

If you believe it's possible for me to see your true form, O Lord of the yogis, then I humbly ask you to reveal your eternal self to me.

Sri Bhagavan said:

Behold, Partha! Countless forms of Mine, radiant and diverse, shining in a multitude of colors and shapes.

Bharata, look at the Adityas, the Vasus, the Rudras, the two Ashvins, and the Maruts. Behold these many wondrous forms, some of which you have never seen before.

Gudakesha, within my body today, I invite you to witness the entire world—all that moves and all that is still—right here in one place. And if there is anything else you wish to see, let it be revealed to you.

You cannot see Me with your human eyes alone, so I will grant you divine vision. Behold now My wondrous power.

Sanjaya said:

After saying this, O King, the boundless Lord of all yogis, whose grace eliminates all sins, revealed to Arjuna his magnificent and all-encompassing form.

The form was an astonishing sight, with countless mouths and eyes, a myriad of wondrous objects, celestial ornaments, and extraordinary weapons all poised for action. Adorned with divine garlands and garments and smeared with a special sandalwood paste, it was a spectacle of endless marvel, stretching in every direction.

Imagine a thousand brilliant suns rising all at once, flooding the sky with light. Even then, their combined radiance wouldn't compare to the brilliance of that great Lord.

In that moment, Pandava saw that within the body of the Lord of all Gods, the entire world was contained in one unified form, yet it appeared in countless distinct ways.

Overwhelmed with awe and with his hair standing on end, Arjuna, bowing deeply with his hands clasped together, said to the Lord.

Arjuna said:

In your body, O Lord, I see all the gods and a multitude of beings. I see Lord Brahma, seated on his lotus throne in his realm, along with all the sages and celestial serpents.

I see you with countless arms, stomachs, mouths, and eyes, manifesting in endless forms from every direction.

You have no end, no middle, and no beginning. You are the Lord of creation, the master of the cosmic form!

I see you as someone wearing a crown, holding a mace and a disc, surrounded by an overwhelming brilliance that shines from every angle. Your radiance is like a blazing fire or the scorching sun, making you impossible to fully grasp or define as a limited being.

I deeply appreciate that you are beyond time and space, boundless and infinite. You are the essence of everything that exists, the ultimate source of the world. You remain constant and unchanging, upholding the eternal truths and principles. You are timeless and whole in every way.

I see you as an eternal presence without a start, middle, or end, brimming with boundless power. Your eyes are like the moon and the sun, and your mouth blazes like a fierce fire, warming and energizing the world with its radiant light.

Truly, you fill every corner of this space between heaven and earth with your presence. Lord, if anyone were to see this incredible, awe-inspiring form of yours, it would make the entire universe shiver with wonder and fear.

Indeed, many kind-hearted people are coming to you. Some, who are feeling scared, are praying with their hands folded. Meanwhile, the sages and enlightened beings, having wished for your well-being, are offering you heartfelt praise and worship.

The Rudras, Adityas, Vasus, Sadhyas, Vishve-Devas, Ashvins, Maruts, Ushmapas, and the countless Gandharvas, Yakshas, Asuras, and Siddhas are all gazing at you in awe and amazement.

O mighty Krishna, as I behold your immense form with countless mouths, eyes, arms, thighs, feet, and stomachs, and your many sharp teeth, I can see that the people are filled with fear—and so am I.

Seeing you, O Lord Vishnu, as a divine being with countless forms, radiant and reaching the heavens, with your wide-open mouth and brilliant eyes, has deeply unsettled me. I find myself lacking the courage and composure to face you.

Looking at your mouths, with their fierce, jutting canines that seem like the flames of destruction, I feel lost and unsettled. Please, O Lord of all gods, bring me peace. You are the Lord in whom the entire world finds its existence.

All of Dhrtarastra's sons, along with many kings, and the great warriors like Bhisma, Drona, and Karna, are rushing into your terrifying mouths, which are full of sharp teeth. Some of them are stuck between your teeth, their heads crushed.

Just like countless rivers flow steadily towards the ocean, so too, these brave souls make their way into your blazing jaws.

And just as moths rush headlong into a blazing flame, so do people rush into your mouths, speeding toward their own destruction.

With your brilliant, fiery mouths, you consume everyone completely, licking your lips repeatedly. Your intense flames fill the whole world with their dazzling light, O Lord Vishnu!

Greetings to you, O Lord, the highest of all gods! I ask you kindly, reveal yourself to me in this awe-inspiring form. Please, show me your true nature, as I am confused and unable to grasp the meaning behind your actions.

Sri Bhagavan said:

I am time, the force that brings an end to all things. I am everywhere, causing people to age and eventually pass away. Even without your involvement, all the warriors gathered here on both sides will eventually come to an end.

So, rise up and make a name for yourself. By defeating your enemies, you will enjoy a thriving kingdom. Those you face have already been vanquished by Me. Just be an instrument of My will, Savyasachin!

May you defeat Drona, Bhisma, Jayadratha, Karna, and the other great warriors who are already doomed by my will. Don't hold back—fight with determination, and you will emerge victorious over your enemies.

Sanjaya said:

Hearing Krishna's words, Arjuna, the prince, with his hands clasped and his body trembling, bowed deeply to Krishna. Overcome by fear, he repeatedly offered his respects and spoke again, his voice shaking with emotion.

Arjuna said:

Indeed, Hrshikesha, it is fitting that the world finds joy and devotion in singing your praises. The fearsome demons scatter in terror, while all the celestial beings bow in reverence to you.

O Lord, the Infinite One! The Sovereign of all Deities! The very essence in which the world exists! How could anyone not bow to You, who are even greater than Brahma, the first creator? You are the eternal, boundless reality, the cause and the result of everything.

You are the highest of the divine beings, existing before all else and encompassing everything. You are the final refuge of the world, both the ultimate knowledge and the knower of all. You are the supreme sanctuary, filling every corner of existence with your boundless presence. O Lord, whose forms are infinite, the entire world is enveloped by you.

You are the master of the air, the ruler of death, the lord of fire and water, You are the presiding deity of the moon, Prajapati, and the supreme great-grandfather, the Creator. I offer you a thousand heartfelt salutations. Again and again, I bow in reverence to you.

Greetings to you in the east and the west, and truly, greetings to you in every direction, O Lord, who embodies everything! You are the source of boundless strength and endless power, completely encompassing all that exists. In essence, you are everything.

Not fully understanding your greatness and thinking of you simply as a friend, I might have spoken lightly, calling you 'O Krishna! O Yadava! O Friend!' out of carelessness or familiarity...

...I might have made light of you, Achyuta, in moments of jest or even in everyday situations—whether while walking, lying down, sitting, eating, or in public. For all of this, I humbly ask for your forgiveness, knowing that you are beyond full comprehension.

O Lord, whose glory knows no equal! You are the father of all beings and objects, both living and non-living, and the most revered teacher of all. In the entire universe, no one compares to you—how could there ever be anyone greater?

I bow deeply and humbly before you, seeking your blessings, O revered Lord. Please forgive my mistakes just as a father would forgive his child, a friend would forgive a friend, or a beloved would forgive their beloved.

O Lord, I am filled with joy upon seeing what I had never seen before. Yet, my heart is also overwhelmed with fear. Please reveal to me only Your original form. Please be kind, O Lord of the Gods, the one in whom the entire world exists!

I hope to see you adorned with a crown, holding a mace and a disc. You, who are the Lord with a thousand arms, embodying the entire world! May you take on the form with just four hands.

Sri Bhagavan said:

Arjuna, I revealed this immense, radiant cosmic form to you through My power, a form that is boundless and encompasses everything, with no end. This vision of Mine is something no one has ever seen before, except for you.

You can't see me through studying the Vedas or performing rituals. Charity, rituals, and severe austerities won't reveal me to anyone else. Only you, Arjuna, the bravest of the Kurus, can see me in this form.

Don't let fear or confusion take hold when you see this intimidating form of mine. Once you've overcome your fear and feel at ease, you'll be able to see my true form once more.

Sanjaya said:

After speaking to Arjuna, Krishna, the son of Vasudeva, revealed his true form once more. He comforted Arjuna, who was frightened, by assuming his divine and reassuring appearance.

Arjuna said:

Janardhana, seeing this beautiful human form of yours has lifted my spirits and brought me back to my true self.

Sri Bhagavan said:

You have witnessed this divine form of Mine, which is incredibly rare to behold. Even the Gods themselves always long to see this form.

I can't be perceived in this form through studying the Vedas, practicing asceticism, giving to charity, or through worship. You are unique in having seen Me in this way.

Arjuna, the mighty warrior, it is through a deep devotion that is unmatched by any other that one can truly come to understand, see, and enter into my divine form.

Arjuna, the person who dedicates all their actions to Me, makes Me their highest priority, is devoted to Me, and is free from attachment and hostility towards others, will find their way to Me.

CHAPTER TWELVE

Devotion

Bhakti Yogah

Arjuna asked:

Among those who are devotedly committed to meditating on you and those who seek you as the eternal, unchanging reality beyond perception, who are the greatest practitioners of yoga?

Sri Bhagavan said:

Those who meditate on Me with unwavering faith and a mind fully devoted, staying ever connected with Me, are regarded by Me as the highest among all.

But those who worship the imperishable, the indefinable, the unmanifested, the all-pervading, the incomprehensible, the immovable, the eternal...

...Through mastering their senses, remaining balanced in all situations, and finding joy in the well-being of all living beings, they too come to Me.

For those who focus on the formless, the path is much harder. It's difficult for people, who are used to living in the physical world, to connect with something they can't see or imagine.

However, those who dedicate all their actions to Me, worship Me with complete devotion, and keep Me as their sole focus—those who are entirely absorbed in Me—I will soon become their guide and liberator from the endless cycle of birth and death.

Place your mind and intellect in Me, and there will be no doubt that you will remain with Me.

If you struggle to keep your mind fixed on Me, Dhananjaya, then try to reach Me through regular practice of yoga (abhyasa yogena).

If you're unable to practice regularly, then just dedicate your actions to Me. By working for My sake, you will still achieve success.

If even that feels too hard, then just surrender the results of all your actions. With self-control, give up attachment to success or failure, and you will find peace.

Jnana is indeed superior to practice (abhyasa); meditation (dhyana) is better than Jnana; and renouncing the results of actions (karma-phala-tyaga) is superior to meditation. Renunciation brings immediate peace.

The person who holds no hatred for anyone, who approaches everyone with a friendly and compassionate attitude, who is free from attachment and ego, and who remains calm and even-tempered in both good and bad times...

...this person, who is truly content, consistently connected, and has control over their mind, whose determination is strong, and whose thoughts and intellect are dedicated to Me, is deeply cherished by Me.

One who is not disturbed by the world and who does not disturb others, who is free from excitement, anger, fear, and anxiety—such a person is dear to Me.

The one who is independent, pure, capable, and balanced; who has overcome fear, abandoned all unnecessary actions, and remains devoted to Me—is dear to Me.

The person who stays composed, is free from hostility, does not grieve or yearn for anything, and has let go of the attachment to both good and bad actions, and who is devoted, is dear to Me.

The person who remains steady in the face of both friends and enemies, honor and disgrace, as well as cold and heat, pleasure and pain, is truly balanced and free from attachment.....

...One who treats praise and blame the same, who is self-controlled and content with whatever they have, who is not attached to a fixed place, and who has a steady mind—such a person is dear to Me.

Those who worship this eternal truth as I have described, with unwavering faith, are very dear to Me.

CHAPTER THIRTEEN

The Known and the Knower

Kshetra-Kshetrajna Vibhaga Yogah

Arjuna said:

Keshava, I really want to understand the nature of prakrti and purusha, the field (kshetra) and the one who knows the field (kshetrajna), as well as the ways of gaining knowledge and what exactly is to be known.

Shri Bhagavan said:

Kaunteya, this body is referred to as the 'field' (kshetra) and the one who understands this 'field' is known as the 'knower of the field' (kshetrajna). This is what those with wisdom say.

O Bharata, recognize Me as the knower within all bodies. True knowledge is understanding both the nature of the body and the one who perceives it. This is the vision I wish to impart.

Now, let me briefly explain what this 'field' is, its nature, its changes, its origins, and the glory of the 'knower of the field.' Listen carefully.

This knowledge is celebrated in various ways by the sages and is reflected in the Vedic texts, which describe it both as diverse and unique. The Vedas, through their statements and reasoning, unequivocally reveal the essence of Brahman.

The 'field' encompasses various aspects: the five subtle elements, the cosmic entity known as Hiranyagarbha, the collective intelligence (samashti-buddhi), the unmanifest cause (maya), the ten organs and the mind, the five sense objects, as well as emotions like desire, aversion, pleasure, and pain. It also includes the physical body, perception, and strength of will. This overview briefly covers the 'field' and its many aspects.

Humility, authenticity, non-harm, adaptability, honesty, dedication to the teacher, cleanliness, mental discipline...

...detachment from sensory pleasures, freedom from arrogance, and a clear understanding of the suffering inherent in birth, death, aging, and illness...

...a deep, unwavering devotion to Me that is not tied to anything else, a preference for solitude, and no desire for socializing...

...constant focus on self-knowledge, always keeping the ultimate goal of understanding the truth in mind- All of these are essential for gaining true knowledge. Anything contrary to these qualities is considered ignorance.

I will clearly explain what is to be known, which, once understood, leads to immortality. This is what is known as Brahman—beginningless, limitless, and neither fully existent as an object nor non-existent.

Brahman is described as having hands and feet in every direction, eyes, heads, and mouths all around, and ears everywhere in all beings, pervading everything.

Though Brahman may seem to have the attributes of physical organs, it is actually beyond all forms and organs, unattached, and the source of everything. It transcends the three gunas of nature but is the experiencer of them.

Brahman exists both within and outside all beings, as something that is unmoving yet also the source of movement. It is subtle and difficult to grasp, being both distant and close.

It remains undivided within all beings, though it may appear divided. It supports and sustains all creation, consuming and creating in turn.

This Brahman, the light of lights, is beyond ignorance. It is pure knowledge, the ultimate truth to be understood, and is present in the minds of all beings.

So, I've briefly explained both the 'field' of knowledge and the process of gaining that knowledge, as well as what is to be known. Anyone who truly understands this and is devoted to Me is prepared to attain unity with Me.

Understand that both prakriti (nature) and purusha (the self) are indeed without beginning. Know that the changes and gunas we see are all manifestations of prakriti.

Prakriti is responsible for creating the physical body and its functions, while purusha is the cause in terms of experiencing pleasure and pain.

Purusha, or the individual self, interacts with prakriti and experiences its attributes. This attachment to these attributes leads to cycles of birth in various forms, whether high or low.

Purusha, the ultimate observer, creator, sustainer, and experiencer, is the limitless self present within the body.

One who comprehends the true nature of purusha and prakriti, along with their attributes, is not bound by rebirth, even while engaging in life's activities.

Some people realize the self through deep contemplation, focusing on the self within the mind and with a prepared mindset. Others achieve this understanding through inquiry, while some do so through the practice of karma-yoga.

However, there are those who, not knowing these methods themselves, learn from teachers and faithfully follow what they've been taught. Even they are able to transcend death.

Bharatarshabha, as long as anything exists—whether moving or stationary—it exists due to the connection between the field (kshetra) and the knower of the field (kshetrajna).

The person who understands that all actions are carried out by prakrti alone, and recognizes the self as merely a witness and not a doer, is the one who truly sees.

When one perceives that the apparent diversity among beings stems from a single, underlying self (Atman), and that these distinctions arise from this singular source, then they attain an understanding of Brahman.

Kaunteya, this boundless self is beginningless and without attributes, making it imperishable. Although it exists within the body, it neither performs actions nor is affected by their outcomes.

Just as space, being subtle and all-pervasive, remains unaffected, the self, which resides in all states of the body, remains unchanged.

Bharata, as a single sun lights up the entire world, so too does the self, which dwells within the body, illuminate the entire field of existence.

Those who grasp the distinction between the field (kshetra) and the knower of the field (kshetrajna) with the eye of wisdom, and who understand the self's freedom from prakrti, the source of all beings, will reach the ultimate truth.

CHAPTER FOURTEEN

The Division of Three Gunas

Gunatraya-Vibhaga-Yogah

Sri Bhagavan said:

I will now explain clearly the highest and most supreme knowledge, the kind that has led all the great sages to ultimate liberation from the cycle of birth and death.

Those who embrace this knowledge and achieve oneness with Me transcend the cycle of rebirth. They are not born again when creation begins, nor do they perish when creation dissolves.

Bharata, my Maya is the primordial force from which everything originates and which sustains all creation. I infuse this energy into the world, leading to the manifestation of all beings.

Kaunteya, my great Maya serves as the original material cause for all forms born in every womb. I am the source that provides the seed, the father.

Arjuna, the mighty-armed one! The three gunas —sattva, rajas, and tamas —that exist in prakrti (nature), bind the eternal self to the physical body.

Arjuna, pure-hearted one, among these gunas, sattva stands out. It is pure, illuminating, and free from affliction. It binds one through a connection to both pleasure and knowledge.

Kaunteya, understand that rajas is like a coloring of the mind, creating desires and deep-seated attachments. It ties the true self in the body to constant activity.

Bharata, know that tamas, born from ignorance, leads to confusion for all who have bodies. It fully binds a person through laziness, indifference, and sleep.

Bharata, sattva binds through pleasure, rajas through action, and tamas through ignorance and lethargy.

Bharata, when sattva prevails, it overcomes both rajas and tamas. Rajas, in turn, overcomes tamas and sattva, while tamas overpowers both rajas and sattva.

When clarity and knowledge shine through all the senses in the body, it indicates that sattva is in control.

Bharatarshabha, when rajas dominates, we experience greed, physical restlessness, active engagement, mental agitation, and strong desires.

On the other hand, when tamas takes over, we become dull, inactive, indifferent, and deluded, O Kurunandana.

When someone who is embodied dies with a predominance of sattva, they attain the higher realms reserved for those who seek the ultimate truth and are free from impurity.

If a person dies with a predominance of rajas, they are reborn among those who are deeply engaged in action. Similarly, if someone dies with a predominance of tamas, they are reborn into situations where discernment is lacking.

It is said that the results of good actions are linked to sattva and bring about pure, distress-free outcomes. On the other hand, actions driven by rajas lead to suffering, and those driven by tamas result in ignorance.

Jnanam arises from the quality of sattva, while greed comes from rajas. Apathy and confusion stem from tamas, as does ignorance.

Those who are primarily influenced by sattva move towards higher realms, those driven by rajas stay in the middle, and those under the influence of tamas, the lowest quality, fall to lower states.

When a person perceives that there is no force acting other than the gunas and understands themselves as being beyond these gunas, they come to truly grasp My nature.

By transcending these three gunas that shape the body, a person becomes free from the cycles of birth, death, aging, and suffering, and achieves immortality.

Arjuna asked:

Lord, what are the traits of someone who has transcended the three gunas? How does such a person behave, and what is the way they rise above these three gunas?

Sri Bhagavan said:

Arjuna, the wise person does not reject brightness, activity, or even delusion when they arise, nor does he yearn for them once they pass.

He remains steady, unaffected by the changing gunas, and understands that these qualities are at work, while he himself stays anchored in his true self.

Such a person treats pleasure and pain, a lump of earth and gold, and pleasant or unpleasant situations with the same equanimity.

He remains the same in the face of praise or criticism, respect or insult, and does not let the opinions of friends or enemies sway him. One who has given up all attachments and actions with an understanding of their true self is considered to be beyond the gunas.

The person who worships Me with unwavering devotion and dedication is truly prepared to realize Brahman, having transcended the gunas.

I am the foundation of Brahman, which is eternal and unchanging. I am the eternal dharma, the underlying truth of everything, and I embody a joy that cannot be diminished or taken away.

CHAPTER FIFTEEN

The Highest Self

Purushottama Yogah

Shri Bhagavan said:

The wise speak of an eternal ashvattha tree with its roots above and branches spreading below, with the Vedas as its leaves. The one who understands this is truly knowledgeable in the Vedas.

Its branches, nourished by the three gunas, spread out above and below, with the sense objects as their offshoots. The roots that extend downward represent actions (karmas), which bind a person in the mortal world.

However, this tree is not perceived as it truly is. It has neither a beginning, an end, nor a stable existence. By using the firm weapon of detachment, one must cut down this deeply rooted ashvattha tree.

Then, one should seek that ultimate destination, from which there is no return, by surrendering to the primal being from whom the entire creation has originated.

Those who have let go of the need for respect and remain objective, who have overcome attachment and are always centered within themselves, free from desires, and unshaken by the dualities of pleasure and pain, reach that eternal destination.

In that place, there is no need for the light of the sun, moon, or fire; once reached, there is no return. That is My boundless abode.

In the realm of living beings, a part of My essence exists as the jiva, which is eternal. When the ruler of the body departs, it gathers the five senses and the mind—its sixth companion—drawing them into itself. As it moves to a new body, it carries these senses and the mind along, much like the wind carries the fragrance from flowers.

Guiding the senses of hearing, sight, touch, taste, and smell, along with the mind, this jiva experiences the world through these sense objects.

Those who are deluded fail to perceive the one who departs from the body, remains in it, or interacts with the world through the gunas. But those with wisdom understand its presence.

The yogis, through their diligent effort, can discern this self manifesting in the intellect. However, those whose minds are immature and lack discernment may not see the true self, even if they are striving.

Understand that the brilliance of the sun that lights up the world, the glow of the moon, and the warmth of the fire all come from Me.

I sustain all living beings by infusing them with strength and nourish the plants by becoming their essence.

I reside in everyone's hearts. From Me come memory, knowledge, and even forgetfulness. I am the ultimate knowledge that the Vedas seek, the source of the Vedanta teachings, and the knower of the Vedas.

There are two types of beings in the world: the perishable (kshara) and the imperishable (akshara). Everything that changes and decays is considered perishable, while the imperishable remains constant and unchanging.

However, there is another, higher being known as the 'Paramatman'—the ultimate self, the infinite and unchanging Lord who upholds and supports the entire universe.

Since I transcend both the perishable and the imperishable, I am celebrated as the Supreme Being, or 'Purushottama', in the world and in the sacred texts.

Whoever, without delusion, understands Me in this way becomes the knower of all and sees Me as the Self of everything, Bharata!

O Bharata, O Anagha! I've shared this deep and profound teaching with you. By understanding this wisdom, a person with true discernment becomes wise and fulfills everything that needs to be accomplished in life.

CHAPTER SIXTEEN

Divine and Demoniac Despositions

Daivasura-Sampad-Vibhaga Yogah

Sri Bhagavan said:

Arjuna, freedom from fear, a pure mind, steady focus in meditation, generosity, self-restraint, performing rituals, reciting one's Vedic texts, practicing religious discipline, and aligning thoughts, words, and actions...

Avoiding harm to others, being truthful, managing anger, renouncing material attachments, focusing the mind, avoiding slander, showing compassion, and not having intense cravings...

Gentleness, modesty, and inner calm, and avoiding physical agitation; brilliance, composure, perseverance, cleanliness, non-violence, and humility—such qualities are inherent in those who are blessed with daivi (divine) qualities.

O Partha! A person born with the traits of an asura (demon) is marked by hypocrisy regarding righteousness, pride, a desire for respect, anger, harshness, and a lack of discernment.

Spiritual wealth leads to liberation, while the traits of an asura lead to entrapment. So, Pandava, do not be disheartened. You are born into spiritual wealth, which guides you towards liberation.

In this world, there are two types of beings: the divine and the demonic. The divine qualities have been discussed extensively. Now, listen, Arjuna, to the characteristics of the demonic beings.

Those who embody demonic qualities are unaware of what should be done or avoided. They lack inner purity, proper behavior, and honesty.

They believe that the world is deceitful, lacking moral foundation, godless, and merely the result of male and female union, driven by passion alone.

Holding onto these views, these enemies of the world—whose minds are clouded, who think narrowly, and who act cruelly—contribute significantly to the world's turmoil and destruction.

People who are driven by difficult-to-attain desires and are plagued by pretension, a craving for respect, and pride often pursue unworthy goals. They are deluded by false ambitions and engage in various actions based on these misguided purposes.

Such individuals are obsessed with their desires until the end of their lives. They focus solely on indulging in their cravings, believing that life is only about these fleeting pleasures. Driven by desire and anger, and trapped by countless hopes, they engage in the unethical accumulation of wealth solely for their personal enjoyment.

They think to themselves, 'Today, I have achieved this. I will also obtain what I desire next. I have this much wealth now, and I will accumulate even more later.'

They think, "I have defeated this enemy, and I will overcome others too. I am the ruler, the enjoyer, the successful, the powerful, and the happy one.

Those who are deeply misguided due to a lack of discernment think, 'I have wealth and was born into a great family. Who is there like me? I will perform rituals, give generously, and enjoy life.'

People who are thoroughly confused by various distractions, trapped in the illusion of their own desires, and completely focused on seeking pleasure from worldly things, end up in places of suffering and pain.

Those who are boasting, vain, and arrogant because of their wealth perform rituals that are merely for show, not following the proper guidelines, driven by pretense.

Those consumed by ego, brute strength, insolence, indulgence, and anger—who look down on Me both in themselves and in others, and who are prone to arguments...

...are hateful and cruel. Such individuals, the lowest among men and wrongdoers, are condemned to repeatedly take birth in demonic realms.

Kaunteya, those who lack discernment and repeatedly take on the nature of asuras with each rebirth, never reach Me. Instead, they end up in an even lower state.

This gateway to suffering, which can lead to a person's downfall, is made up of three things: desire, anger, and greed. Therefore, it's important to let go of these three destructive forces.

Kaunteya, when someone is free from these three dark influences, they follow a path that is truly beneficial for themselves and ultimately reach a higher state.

On the other hand, a person driven by unchecked desire who disregards the guidance of sacred texts will not achieve growth or happiness in this life, let alone reach a higher goal.

Therefore, the scriptures are your guide, Arjuna, for understanding what should and shouldn't be done. By following their teachings, you can navigate your actions in this world correctly.

CHAPTER SEVENTEEN

Three Types of Faith

Shraddha-Traya-Vibhaga Yogah

Arjuna asked:

Krishna, what about those who follow rituals with great faith but ignore what the scriptures prescribe? What motivates them—are they influenced by sattva, rajas, or tamas?

Sri Bhagavan said:

The faith of embodied beings reflects the nature of their minds and comes in three types: sattvic, rajasic, and tamasic. Let me explain these three types of faith.

Arjuna, the type of faith each person has is in harmony with their mind. A person is shaped by their faith, and they act according to it.

Sattvic individuals worship the gods; rajasic people worship spirits and supernatural beings, while tamasic individuals turn to ghosts and lower entities.

People who are driven by pretense and ego, lacking in discernment, and consumed by intense passion and desire, may engage in severe and misguided religious practices not prescribed by the scriptures. They inflict suffering on their senses and on themselves, and even on Me, who dwells within them—know that such individuals are of asura conviction.

For everyone, the type of food they prefer reflects their nature, and the same goes for rituals, discipline, and charity. These preferences can be categorized into three types. Here's how they differ:

Sattvic people are drawn to foods that are fresh, rich, and nourishing—foods that promote longevity, clarity of mind, strength, health, and a pleasing taste. These foods are enjoyed for their taste and their ability to enhance well-being.

Rajasic people favor foods that are bitter, sour, salty, overly spicy, or pungent—foods that can cause discomfort, distress, or health issues. They are attracted to foods that create a strong sensory impact.

Tamasic people prefer food that is stale, poorly cooked, or spoiled—foods that are old, decomposed, or unsuitable as offerings. They are drawn to foods that lack vitality and nourishment.

A ritual that is carried out with a mindset of purity, as prescribed by the scriptures, and performed without expecting any result other than the purification of the mind, is considered sattvika.

In contrast, a ritual performed with the goal of achieving a specific outcome or merely to showcase one's own piety is known as rajasika, O Bharatashreshtha!

A ritual that ignores scriptural guidelines, lacks proper offerings, does not include the recitation of mantras, and is devoid of faith, is regarded as tamasika.

Worshipping deities, brahmanas, teachers, and wise individuals, maintaining physical cleanliness, being straightforward, practicing self-discipline, and avoiding harm to others—all these are considered the discipline of the body.

Discipline of speech includes speaking in a way that is calm, truthful, pleasant, and beneficial, along with regularly reciting one's own Vedic texts.

Mental discipline involves maintaining a cheerful attitude, expressing happiness, avoiding the pressure to speak unnecessarily, mastering the mind, and having pure intentions.

The threefold tapas (austerity/discipline), when performed with sincere devotion by those who seek only mental purity and maintain composure, is known as sattvika tapas.

The type of tapas done with the intention of gaining honor, respect, and praise, and done in a showy manner, is known as rajasika. This kind of tapas is unstable and doesn't last.

On the other hand, tapas that arises from misguided understanding—such as inflicting hardship on oneself or harming others—is called tamasika.

Charity given with the intention of not expecting anything in return, at the right time, in the right place, and to a deserving person, is considered sattvika charity. This type of charity is given with the pure intention, 'It is the right thing to do.'

In contrast, charity given with the hope of receiving something in return, or with the expectation of future rewards (such as spiritual merit or punya), and that which involves effort or discomfort, is considered rajasika charity.

Charity that is given disrespectfully, at an inappropriate time or place, and to undeserving recipients, is known as tamasika charity.

'Om tat sat' represents the three aspects of Brahman. It was by this expression that the Brahmanas, the Vedas, and the rituals were initially created.

For those familiar with the Vedas, activities such as rituals, charity, and religious practices always begin with the utterance of 'Om'.

When performing various activities like rituals, religious practices, and charity, those seeking liberation (moksha) do so with the understanding that these actions are meant to purify the self, rather than seeking any specific results.

The term 'sat' is used to signify both the act of bringing something into existence and living a righteous life. Similarly, Partha, the term 'sat' is applied to actions performed with a sense of purity and sanctity.

Commitment to rituals, religious practices, and acts of charity is called 'sat', and actions done for the sake of these purposes (or for the sake of the Lord) are also referred to as 'sat'.

On the other hand, actions performed without faith—whether rituals, charity, or religious practices—are considered 'asat'. These actions, which do not fulfill their intended purpose, are fruitless both in this life and after death.

Freedom and Renunciation

Moksha-Sannyasa Yogah

Arjuna said,

Hrshikesha, the slayer of Kesi, and mighty-armed one! I wish to clearly understand the true meaning of sannyasa (renunciation) and tyaga (relinquishment).

Sri Bhagavan said:

The wise understand sannyasa as the renunciation of actions driven by personal desires, while the learned people define tyaga as the renunciation of the results of all actions.

Some wise individuals believe that actions, being inherently flawed, should be given up altogether. Others argue that certain actions, such as rituals, charity, and religious practices, should never be abandoned.

Arjuna, the wisest of the Bharata family, and a true tiger among men, listen to my clear perspective on renunciation. There are three kinds of renunciation, and it's important to understand them.

You should not give up actions like rituals, charity, or spiritual practices; these must indeed be carried out. These actions are purifying for those who seek wisdom.

However, even these actions should be performed without attachment and without concern for the results. This is My clear and correct perspective, Partha!

It is not right to renounce duties that are prescribed. If someone abandons these duties out of confusion or ignorance, that is considered tamasika renunciation.

If someone gives up their actions because they find them physically challenging or out of fear of discomfort, that kind of renunciation is called rajasika. Such renunciation does not lead to the true benefits of renunciation.

However, when someone performs their duties with the mindset of 'This must be done', without attachment to the action or its results, that is considered sattvika renunciation, the highest form.

A true renunciate, someone who has let go of attachment to the results of their actions, is a person with a pure mind. With clear understanding and no lingering doubts, they neither reject difficult tasks nor become attached to pleasant ones.

While it's not possible to completely avoid actions as long as one has a physical body, a true renunciant is someone who has let go of attachment to the results of their actions and is known as a 'tyagin'.

The threefold result of action—unpleasant, pleasant, and mixed—comes to those who are attached to the fruits of their actions. But for those who have renounced the results of actions, no such results follow, neither in this world nor in the next.

Listen carefully, Arjuna, to these five factors that contribute to the completion of any action, as described in the Vedanta, which represents the culmination of all knowledge about karma.

These five factors are: the physical body, the agent (or person performing the action), the various means of action, the different activities of the vital energies (pranas), and the presiding deities, or divine forces.

These five elements come into play in every action performed by body, speech, or mind, whether it is righteous or not.

However, someone who mistakenly sees the self, which is pure, as the doer due to an immature mind, will not grasp the truth correctly.

A person who understands that they are not the true doer and remains unaffected by actions—such a person, even if they were to kill, does not actually kill nor are they bound by their actions.

Knowledge, the object of knowledge, and the knower together drive action. Similarly, the means of action, the object of action, and the agent are the three components of action.

According to the scriptures that discuss the gunas (qualities), knowledge, action, and the agent are categorized into three types based on their gunas. Here's a brief overview:

Sattvika knowledge is the understanding that sees the unchanging essence in all things and recognizes the unity within the diversity.

Rajasa knowledge, on the other hand, perceives the world as being made up of distinct, separate entities, focusing on their varied nature.

Tamasa knowledge is fixated on a single object as if it represents everything, often leading to confusion, lack of truth, and limited understanding.

An action done according to prescribed duties, without attachment or personal desires, and without being swayed by likes or dislikes, is considered sattvika.

An action driven by strong desires for specific outcomes or done with arrogance and excessive effort is called rajasa.

An action that is started without considering the natural consequences, potential harm, or one's own limitations, and is done out of ignorance or delusion, is referred to as tamasa.

A person who is detached, free from ego, and driven by determination and enthusiasm, remaining calm in both success and failure, is considered a sattvika doer.

A person who is driven by desire, seeking results, greedy, harmful, unclean, and fluctuates between elation and depression is known as a rajasika doer.

A person who is troubled, immature, disrespectful, deceptive, cruel, lazy, prone to sadness, and prone to procrastination is identified as a tamasika doer.

Dhananjaya, listen carefully to the three types of mind and resolve, as categorized by the three gunas, which I will explain in detail.

A mind that understands what actions to pursue and what to avoid, what to fear and what not to fear, and the difference between bondage and freedom, is considered sattvika.

A mind that misinterprets what is proper and improper, and confuses what should and shouldn't be done, is rajasika.

A mind that, clouded by ignorance, sees what is wrong as right and everything in reverse, is tamasika.

A steadfast resolve that supports the consistent practice of mind control, breath regulation, and the functioning of the senses is known as sattvika resolve, Partha.

In contrast, a resolve driven by the desire for results, which motivates one to pursue actions for religious merit, pleasure, or security as opportunities arise, is called rajasika resolve, Partha.

Lastly, a resolve characterized by improper thinking, which fails to overcome excessive sleep, fear, sorrow, depression, and intoxication, is termed tamasika resolve, Partha.

Now, listen, Bharatarshabha, as I explain the three types of happiness. The happiness that comes from regular practice and leads to the end of sorrow,...

...though it may seem bitter at first but turns sweet with time—is known as sattvika. This happiness arises from a clear understanding of the self.

The happiness derived from sensory experiences, which feels delightful at the start but becomes bitter as time passes, is called rajasika.

The happiness that feels deceiving and is rooted in laziness, sleep, and apathy, both at the beginning and the end, is referred to as tamasika.

No being, whether on Earth or among the gods in heaven, is free from these three gunas that arise from nature (prakrti).

O Parantapa, the duties of the brahmanas, kshatriyas, vaishyas, and shudras are each determined by the qualities that come from one's inherent nature, divine influence, and actions.

For a brahmana, the duties are centered around qualities such as composure, self-restraint, religious discipline, cleanliness (both internal and external), adaptability, righteousness, knowledge, and a deep respect for the Vedas.

A kshatriya's natural duties include valor, self-confidence, determination, skillfulness, facing challenges without retreat, generosity, and leadership.

The vaishyas are naturally inclined towards agriculture, animal husbandry, and trade, while the shudras are naturally suited for service and support roles.

These duties arise naturally from one's qualities and are integral to maintaining harmony and fulfilling one's role in society.

A person who takes joy in fulfilling their own duty finds true success. Let me explain how someone devoted to their responsibilities can achieve this.

By performing their own duty and dedicating their actions to that divine source from which all beings arise and which pervades everything, a person attains success.

Even if your own duty seems imperfect, it is still better than the well-executed duty of someone else. By following your own path and acting according to your nature, you avoid any faults or blemishes.

Kaunteya, even if your natural duties have imperfections, don't abandon them. All endeavors have their flaws, much like fire has smoke.

The person who remains unattached everywhere, has control over their mind, and has overcome all desires, achieves the highest state of actionlessness through renunciation.

Kaunteya, learn from Me briefly how one, who has attained this inner purity (antahkarana-shuddhi), reaches Brahman, the supreme knowledge.

A person with a clear mind, who controls their body, mind, and senses with firm determination, and who relinquishes desires for sensory pleasures like sounds and tastes...

...someone who lives in solitude, eats modestly, and has mastery over their speech, body, and mind; who is dedicated to meditation and free from craving...

...such a person, who abandons ego, power, vanity, possessiveness, anger, and a sense of ownership over external things, and remains serene, is well-prepared to attain the knowledge of Brahman as their true self.

A person who has recognized themselves as Brahman—whose mind is serene and free from grief or longing—sees all beings as equal to themselves. Such a person attains the highest devotion to Me.

Through this devotion, they understand My true nature and, having grasped this reality, they merge with Me.

A person who consistently performs righteous actions with Me as the foundation, and whose ultimate goal is union with Me, will attain the eternal and imperishable end by My grace.

By dedicating all actions to Me and embracing a life of buddhi-yoga, make yourself one whose mind is always centered on Me.

When your mind is constantly aligned with Me, you will overcome all challenges with My grace. But if you let ego stand in your way and refuse to listen, you will face ruin.

If you let your ego tell you, 'I won't fight', this decision is misguided. Your natural tendencies will ultimately drive your actions.

Kaunteya, out of confusion and being bound by your inherent nature, you will end up doing exactly what you don't want to do, despite your intentions.

Arjuna, the Lord resides within the intellect of all beings, guiding them with His divine power (Maya), like a machine making figures spin.

Give yourself entirely to Him with a full heart, Bharata! Through His grace, you will find lasting peace and reach the eternal sanctuary.

I have shared with you the most profound and hidden knowledge. Reflect on this deeply, and then choose your path as you see fit.

Listen carefully to My final and most profound teaching, which is the deepest secret of all. Because you are so dear to Me, I will share what is truly beneficial for you.

Surrender your mind to Me, direct your devotion towards Me, and worship Me. By doing so, you will come to Me alone. I promise this to you because you are cherished by Me.

Give up all your actions and take refuge solely in Me. I will free you from all your karma; do not worry or grieve.

This teaching should not be shared with those who lack discipline, devotion, willingness to listen, or those who criticize Me without reason.

But whoever teaches this most sacred wisdom to My devotees, with the highest devotion to Me, will surely come to Me. There is no doubt about this.

Among all those who act according to My will, no one is dearer to Me than the one who shares this knowledge, and no one will ever be dearer on this earth.

Anyone who studies or recites this conversation of ours, which upholds righteousness, is performing a ritual of knowledge (Jnana Yajna), and through this, they are worshipping Me. This is My firm conviction.

Anyone who has faith in this teaching and does not criticize it, even if they simply listen to it, will be freed from the cycle of rebirth and attain the blessed realms of those who perform good deeds.

Partha, have you listened to this with a focused mind? Has the confusion caused by ignorance been cleared, Dhananjaya?

Sanjaya said:

I have heard this profound and awe-inspiring conversation between Krishna and Arjuna, two souls of great wisdom and heart, a dialogue so moving that it sends shivers down my spine.

Thanks to the grace of Vyasa, I was able to listen to this secret and highest form of yoga, directly taught by Krishna, the Lord of Yoga, himself.

O King! As I keep remembering this incredible and blessed exchange between Krishna and Arjuna, I find myself filled with joy, over and over again.

Moreover, each time I remember the awe-inspiring form of Lord Hari, I am overwhelmed with amazement and joy, O King!

Wherever Krishna, the Lord of yoga, is present, and wherever Arjuna, the mighty archer, stands, there will always be prosperity, victory, abundance, and righteousness. This is my firm belief.

Om Tat Sat

This concludes the reading of Shrimad Bhagavad Gita, a dialogue between Sri Krishna and Arjuna. It captures the essence of the Upanishads, exploring both the knowledge of Brahman and the practice of Yoga.

About The Author

Naveen Niverthy is passionate about spirituality and self-realization, studying Vedanta with a traditional teacher for almost 10 years, despite being a sales and marketing professional with a mechanical engineering degree. He believes in holistic development and empowering individuals to achieve happiness across physical, emotional, spiritual, and intellectual aspects, while positively impacting their family, work, and social lives.

He is the author of 'Think Better and Thrive' and 'Step by Step: A Guide to Achieving Your Goals in Five Moves'. He regularly blogs at naveenniverthy.com, sharing insights on balancing various life pursuits.